HOUSE OF ANGELS
BY LOMAN BELL

House of Angels

It started as a journey, seeking for adventure,
Looking through the darkness, for things to satisfy.
Trusting only in my passions, strayed from the path,
Trying to climb the mountain, unsure of steps on the way.

The night I spent, in the house of angels,
No one seemed to be, whom you expected to see;
Out of the darkness I ran, with terror through the night,
Not sure if the next step was wrong or was right.

Encounter with evil, not sure the reason why,
I know I'd been slipping, from the sweet by and by;
Then came the confrontation, can I make it on my own;
You heard my cry, thank You Jesus, You, sent holy angels from Your throne.

Oh God, my heart is crying, come by here and save me now,
The darkness is all around me, can't see! I'm falling down;
There's no other name to call, I know your power has no end.
Your angels came, helped me through it; You're my God, You're my friend.

House of Angels

Copyright 2009 by Loman Bell
Publisher: Wood Islands Prints
670 Trans-Canada Highway, RR 1
Belle River, PEI C0A 1B0, Canada

Credits:

The painting on page 10 is taken from Mr. Bell's childhood Bible; it has proved impossible to identify a copyright holder, but credit will be given in future editions, if notified.

Dedication:

Dedication

I wish to dedicate this book to the best parents in the whole world, who lovingly raised me with a deep respect for God and His Word. Also they showed me by example and their ability how to work hard and love it. They showed me that even though it may be hard times, we have it within ourselves to get by. There's a way within us; if we keep looking and searching we will find contentment, with the basic fact that God's love is in us. For sure, I don't regret any one of the times they took me to church, especially my mother, taking me, where I found the path to eternal life with all its blessings. I sure appreciate my dad, my best friend too, who showed by example how not to worry about getting your hands dirty to get the job done. I don't believe there were two better parents in the whole world, this side of heaven. I can only try to be like them. Above all else, they showed me the direction to God. This is where, with their help, I had the opportunity to be born again.

First Family Picture

House of Angels

My Parents

Table of Contents

Dedication .... *iii*

Table of Contents .... *v*

Poems & Songs .... *vii*

Introduction 1
    Threads of My Life 1
    In The Beginning 5

God Sends Angels 9
    Saved From Death 13
    Narrow Bridge 21
    Out From Under The Truck 25

My Early Years 30
    Parents 30
    Horses 33
    Growing Up 36
    Winters 41
    Too Young to Chop Trees 43
    Bike Excitement 44
    Water Fun 46
    Murray River Ships 48
    Job Displacement 51
    Church Influences 53
    Old Fashioned Church 55
    Evangelistic Rallies 61

    Other Church Activities 64
    Music Influences 68
    My Guitar 70

Wanderings 72
    Bible College 72
    Jail Time 74
    Close Calls 75
    Drink 77
    Bible College Again 78
    Out West To Work 79
    Vancouver 80
    Party Encounters—Wild Kind 82
    Through The Rockies Heading Home 87
    Back Home 94
    On The Road Again 95
    Back Home Again 100

Thoughts 101
    I Can't Help But Share 101
    Hope 102
    Nature Of Man 104
    The Judgement 108
    Prayer And Meditation 113
    God Sees Us 114
    Living God and Resurrection Power 116

Conclusion 118
    The Goal 118

Poems & Songs:

Poems & Songs

House of Angels i
Thy Will Be Done 1
One Day 2
Highway Of Life 4
I Remember A Time 6
Yes Victory 20
Moving Along 22
Hope 24
Free Free Free 29
This Precious Jesus 54
Running the Race 57
Jesus My Friend 59
The Ransom Paid 62
Giving Thanks 63
On The Shore Of Destiny 73
In The Valley Of Decision 76
Lost Or Found 85
Journey On 93
Determined 98
I Love You 103
Hoping 106
Pathway To Home 107
Amazing God 107
Gonna Climb That Mountain 108
Living Eternally 110
He Shall Return 112
Power Prayer 113
Thy Face Oh Lord 117
I'll Serve Jesus 118
The Hand Of God 119
Earth's Final Sundown 120
After All 123

House of Angels

Introduction

Threads of My Life

As I write this, I'm trying to follow a pathway weaving through my entire life. This is God's care. I thank God for it! I see how everything was connected, through the church, my music, and my wanderings my whole life long. There it was in the places I went, the people I've known, and the good and bad events in my life. In this book, I relate some of these times when the lifeline of God's care was most evident.

Thy Will Be Done

I thank you Lord, for all You've done,
For sending Jesus, Your only Son,
To die upon, cruel Calvary;
I thank you lord, for saving me.

Dear Jesus I pray, it is Your will what I say,
What I do, what I think,
To have a passion for You. To be what I am.
I know that it is God, who has this whole world in His
    hands;

Teach me Lord how to pray,
To follow You and Your pathway,
For me and for others, always we'll see
Our life is in You, without You, it's empty.

Let me care for others, as You have done;
I know Your love, is the only true one.
Carrying through the roughest trials, we know
Eternal life through You, Lord, to show.

On You may my eyes, always want to be,
Fixed and secured, till that coming day
When by grace we will finally, be able to hear,
"Well done, faithful servant," these words so clear.

House of Angels

My stories include times when God or His holy angels worked miracles in my life. They work everywhere in the world for good and justice, peace and rest, and especially truth and wisdom. This presence of these holy beings seemed evident everywhere by their action, the results of our prayers, and the outcome of certain events. Even today through our awareness of God, His presence, and His love for mankind, there is a vast intervention of His holy power involving Angels, who will work on the behalf of mankind, weaving through the pathways, a person would travel. Our Heavenly Father's care being demonstrated throughout our lives, and especially now I can see and feel this wonderful intervention that was there all the time and still is there working on behalf of mankind.

One Day
Standing with the choices at hand,
Looking out o'er creation, everything so grand,
Knowing God the Creator, made this world for man,
Then while we are living in it, giving us a hand.

There is this one choice, a broad road so vast,
With only a pit in the end to be cast,
There is also this other choice, narrow and clear,
With the son shining always, from God's home so near.

See into the future, eternity for man-
All of the people, where will they stand?
Looking towards Jesus, His love we will greet,
face all life's problems, and place at His feet.

No matter what I do, or where I may go,
I have only to choose and let it show,
And friends who are with us towards eternity grand,
Must depend on Jesus, hold to his helping hand.

I believe from our very beginning, as a human being, God moulds and shapes us for the path we have to walk through life. All of this depends extremely close on our child-

Introduction: Threads of My Life

hood training and the teaching and instruction we receive. If we're blessed with parents who show us faith, the circumstances don't break our spirit.

Weaving throughout my whole life I've seen such amazing intervention from God, His unbeatable power, and the resources He has readily available, like His angels, prayer warriors, and Christians who are involved in, throwing out the lifeline, like the words of the old hymn says.

When we take the time searching for the truth in events and thoughts like these, there appear outstanding facts. Come along and see for yourself, God is there all the time, to hell and back, and capable of letting His overpowering presence be known, through the good times and the bad, anytime He chooses.

He's Coming Again

So first off I'll get right down to it and give a first hand view, first hand of God's intervention, up close and personal, on behalf of us mere human beings. Then later on I'll talk a little about my life, where I was born, with some history and interesting facts about the area. At the closing of this time together, I would like to talk from my heart, the things of conscience, believing still in God today.

Highway Of Life

Travelling on the highway of life,
Travelling on, in the daytime and the night.
There's many rough spots, on this road,
But I don't want to carry no heavy load.
Since Jesus came and lives within my heart,
He will always make those bad times depart.
While I'm travelling on this highway of life,
I know He'll always help us stay satisfied.

If I will yield full control of the wheel,
To Jesus, God's Son, and soon coming King,
He lives inside my heart, and helps me sing.
Glory hallelujah all the way.
Since He saved my soul,
I'll give Him full control.
Now I'll yield to Him, my best friend,
And travel on this highway through life.

Won't you come along with me right now my friend?
Jesus will be with us 'til our journey's end.
While we travel on this highway, here below,
Knowing one day to heaven, we will go.
Jesus will guide us all the way on the road,
If we're keeping a heavenly home as our goal.
As we're travelling with Jesus day and night,
Give Him control, and He'll always guide you right.

There's no missing piece in this puzzle
As we're travelling on the highway of life.
I'm a changed man since I met the Lord.
There are no missing pieces in this puzzle
As we're travelling on the highway of life.

I didn't have any regrets for the decision I made to do

Introduction: In The Beginning

Highway of Life

my best to live for God through the good times and bad, through the mountaintops and the valleys. Now forward into eternity, I'm attempting to show this thread weaving through my life, in church, daily living, my journeys, and adventures, at home and abroad, in music—in any abilities I may have. I'm not trying to make God or his Holy Angels into just a story, though—they're so much more awesome and majestic than that. God's visits into our dimension are amazing. God gets involved in man's affairs when He chooses. We humans are so fragile and perishable. I hope, in this book, you will see beyond the simple things of life and see the amazing power of God.

In The Beginning

When I think about God, who He is, and what He is, it is just an overwhelming experience. I feel His power is unlimited and creation would be a small feat for Him with all His abilities. He is, omniscient, omnipotent and omnipresent. The way He may have begun the whole universe seems to me, something like this.

In the beginning of time, as we know it being recorded, God created all things by His hands, by the words of His mouth. He made all things

House of Angels

> ### I Remember A Time
>
> I remember a time when flowers could sing,
> The words about youth, their sweet voices ring.
> Then came the growing excitement and pain,
> Remembering youth looking for the rain.
>
> I remember a time when it seemed to stand still,
> Even then the flowers, would sing as well,
> Seasons would stay just as they should be,
> Flowers would grow, blooms we could see.
>
> I remember a time seems to fly day by day,
> Looking towards tomorrow, the flowers song would say;
> So cheer up my voice, join in with the song;
> Even life seems to pass, and takes us along.

When Flowers Could Sing

    Out of this great mass, He spun pieces everywhere throughout this universe, all of it being part of the original mass. He spoke into existence this hot, burning, flaming,

Introduction: In The Beginning

chaotic, rumbling, exploding matter. These little pieces were part of and similar to the original created mass. God set them in the sky to reflect the sun's rays as stars in the night sky. Other pieces were comets, meteors, asteroids, and other pieces of matter, all of the other being parts of what we may see in the night sky passing by, revolving endlessly through this massive creation Made by God speaking and forming into an orderly fashion, sequencing the beginning of time with nature and eventually His earth for His people (the Garden of Eden). All the earth, in its first state, full of so much beauty and plenty.

The earth was being created, massive, void, dark and chaotic, with all the rest of this burning, trembling, exploding mass, being shaped by the never- ending power of God.

With the greater light (the sun) to rule the day and the lesser light (the moon) to rule the night.

Then the Spirit of the Lord, (this omnipotent creator) moved upon the face of the deep. Mountains being broken, smashing, tumbling, volcanoes erupting, wind so strong ripping the rocks apart; landslides smashing rocks, tumbling, cracking. Water rushing, thrashing, cooling. Condensing, all as part of the original forces of nature in their original forming and shaping the then- new earth, with this power unleashed by God like a bomb. All things exploding, changing mass, structure forming and rearranging all things, cooling lava (hot molten rock ingredients), rumbling earthquakes, tidal force waves thundering around the globe with storm force hurricanes, tornadoes, showing the perfect original creation power and force needed for creation, unlimited and unmatched.

Then the Spirit of the Lord God breathed upon the face of the deep (the surface of the earth) bringing peace, and the framing of the peaceful earth (as we know it) had begun. The seeding of these massive trees in all their beauty. The sweet multiple, fragrant, blossoming flowers; edible seed-bearing grasses and grains; springs and water flowing to water the earth for fruitful production. Even if our mortal minds will try, how can our abilities ever compare even in thought to such an awesome creative power? So when I began my journey in life, I was made aware early of a God, the one and only true God, and of His massive power and abilities. So when it comes time to go on this road of life, through our mental and physical choices, I believe we determine where we will live forever. By these choices we make I believe we can determine where is the end of this earth's journeys when our road will end, at least on this physical travel here, before He gives us our immortal transformation, when then we will live forever like Him and with Him to enjoy all the pleasures of heaven forevermore. May we always be in the presence of Almighty God, waiting His homecoming, because we choose to live with and for Him! Definitely while here below He will and does send His holy angels to help and intervene on our behalf. Though our journey takes us down many different roads, He can be right there in an instant to deliver if we call out His name; "Oh! God, in Jesus Name come and help me, Lord". The best intercontinental travel, God's almighty power connecting with man, and visiting us here on earth, by His presence, and, or, His mighty Angels, coming to intervene on our behalf. I'm a changed man since I met the Lord.

God Sends Angels

It all started when I was very young, in Sunday school, hearing the Bible stories about the beginning of man, about God, about angels and all the ways they interacted with man. I remember some specific stories, like *Jacob's ladder.* Genesis: 28,10-22. The story maybe could have been like this. Maybe it was a cloudy night out on the trail herding his flocks, lying on the bed mat resting with one eye open, looking for the wolves, and suddenly from the sky a giant ladder appears; down the ladder come these angels, descending from the Lord. An Angel met him there resulting in an encounter. Jacob seeks a blessing from the Angel, and God blesses him with land, and prosperity, for him, his descendants, and all the people of the earth, and He would never leave them, Jacob calls that place Bethel. Can you imagine what we would do just to meet a heavenly being, and what questions would be going through our minds? Have they come today to bring God's blessings in our lives? Could they be here to answer a prayer? Yet with all this activity and the holy visitation going on right here in front of Jacob, it must have been a challenge to stay focused and alert.

Again in Gen. 32:22-31, a second encounter when Jacob is met by a heavenly being, sent from God. The Angel blessed him there, resulting in the name of the place being called, Peniel. *("Because I saw God face to face")*, this led him into a whole night of wrestling with the Angel, seeking for a blessing. The end being, Jacob was blessed, but also with a hip out of joint as a sign of the long night of wrestling with the angel.

Another appearance I heard about in Sunday School was when the angel told Mary (Jesus' mother) the baby she was to give birth to, was the Son Of God.

Another visit of a heavenly kind was when Jesus was dead and lay in the tomb. After the stone was rolled away the first day of the week, an angel was on guard, sitting on the stone. His appearance was like lightning, and his clothes were white as snow. When the women approached him, he said to them, *"Do not be afraid, for I know that you are look-*

Jacob's Dream

ing for Jesus, who was crucified, He is not here; He has risen,

God Sends Angels : In The Beginning

just as He said. Come and see the place where He lay."

These are just a very few of the many recorded times when these heavenly beings had an encounter with man. In the Bible we read, *"Are not all angels ministering spirits sent to serve those who will inherit salvation?"* (Hebrews 1:13,14). In addition, there are references to angels in Joshua 10:24 and Psalms 103:20. So as far back as I can remember, I heard these Bible references to angels.

Throughout my life, especially after being saved at age seven (accepting what Jesus did at Calvary and confessing that I believed, and that God has raised Him from the dead), I have been taught about the presence of angels everywhere and how they are involved with the affairs of mankind. I believe for sure there have been many times personally when the outcome of accidents or problems could have had a very different result, were it not for the help of God and His holy angels.

What an overwhelming idea that God in heaven would send angelic messengers to man. Through the entire Bible, Old Testament to New, they appear as messengers, warriors, deliverers, comforters, like the verse, *"His angels, are they not ministering servants sent forth to minister to those who are heirs of salvation?"* To us who have been born again we have been born into this heavenly family, where our Father in heaven cares about His children so much He would send His angels to help and perform all these other wonderful things on our behalf. It really makes you feel important to our heavenly Father, We, just a product of the 'dust of the earth', having been given life by His breath breathed into us, are now inheriting all the wonderful promises and blessings of God—both here and eventually in heaven some day, home by our Father's side. One of the all-time favourite verses of mine, especially when having been introduced to God and his people praising Him with their whole hearts, and serving Him is, *"The angel of the Lord encamps round about those who fear Him."*

I remember when very young hearing people say things like, "Children talk to angels," or, "It must have been an angel helped them get out of that situation," referring to a bad sickness or an accident.

This must be where, the thread, the connecting of all these circumstances in my life started off—with the awareness of these wonderful angelic beings who can intervene on our behalf. The pathway in life, with all its choices, begins at the very beginning, and even before, in God's master plans. So it weaves its way through our whole existence, pointing always to God for authorship. Day by day, week by week, year by year, its all in His hands. Then looking back and observing where we came from, it seems like a line through our entire life, influenced by God, along with all the choices we make. Yet all the time realizing angels always do what they do for God and serve Him in their actions.

Childhood Friends

We all know that children usually don't know too much about dangers, and so when I think back to early childhood, it amazes me that I wasn't involved in more troubles than I was. Most of the time I didn't mind travelling alone—even at ages 2, 3, and 4. I'd get in my cart and push it up and down Main Street, on the sidewalk just inches away from these big 3-ton trucks hauling gravel up and down the street. I can

God Sends Angels : Saved From Death

still remember the roar as they went zooming past us gearing down for the hill. I recall, all the times we played around the river on rafts, dories, or just swimming—no adults watching us—just us kids.

I believe that all this time God in heaven was watching and caring about us children playing there. I believe He still cares about children everywhere and I only want to give praise and thanks to Him.

Saved From Death

Entering Edmonton

One of the three most memorable times I've encountered real interventions was when I was out west looking for work. I was staying at an apartment, running out of money in Edmonton, Alberta. One morning I heard about a day-work place downtown, where you could drop in and sign up for a job. So of I went, signed up, and got placed for a tear-down job on the other side of town in an industrial area. I used the last 25¢ I had to purchase a bus ticket. I landed at the job site and discovered just an old wore down bunch of buildings, where I was directed to one specific building. It looked like it could fall down at any time—a rusty metal building with a couple of vehicles around it. I approached the place and met a grumpy, cross individual that showed me wrenches, and ladders—we were to tear it down. It was a kind of prefabricated smaller building inside this old warehouse. So we just undid the bolts and nuts, putting them in a container, and removing panel type sheets of this little building. The day's work went by, and I went downtown to the main office to be paid the few dollars for the job.

Sketch of Warehouse Job

Where I got the money, they kept some and paid the rest—about 50 -70%. I didn't like the feel of working in that place, so I determined to not go back the next day, but look for another job. In the meantime, I went downtown that day and bought some food, etc.—all the things you would do after waiting for some money and finally getting it. I spent the rest of the day into the night walking around. On the way to my apartment, walking down a street that was the area for the "night businesses" like the Turkish baths, Chinatown, etc., a van drives along the street. When it passed me on the opposite side of the street, it stopped, turned around, pulled along, just ahead of where I was walking, and stopped. Out jumped two guys—one was the fellow I met at the day-job the day before. I believe he was the boss or foreman of that job where we were tearing down those old buildings. They sure didn't seem to be very happy. He came over to me and started this conversation about, "Where was I from?" And when he determined I was from the East Coast, he then started talking ignorantly like, "The East Coast, everything there is rusty, nothing is worth anything," and so on, just running the East down, trying to start a fight. So of course I felt this just didn't sound right and responded, "Don't give me this grease talk man," and then the next step was scuffle time, I had just finished about a 15 hour hike, worn out, tired, and there were two of them. Then to top it all off, one guy snapped a shotgun from under his trench coat and loaded it. Hearing this loading and cocking of the gun was enough to make me feel like I was not in the right place. Then he pointed it. The other guy measured me up with this martial arts stance and, before I knew it, I flew through the air and landed on my butt about 6-8 feet out in the street. With a quick shake I immediately realized that this was not going the way of a peaceful solution. I jumped up and took off, fleeing towards an intersection where there was a bunch of traffic stopping and driving. Approaching the vehicles, I knocked on the windows and after getting their attention, I asked them for a drive—someone was after me, and I believed they were trying to kill me. Of course, at three in the morning, seeing someone running down the street, it would not seem to be the safest thing, to let them in your vehicle.

With no help and everyone driving away, the only choices were to stop and face these guys who were trying to kill me or seek another exit. The latter sounded better so off I went again in a steady sprint, and panicked, hearing those footsteps closing in. And of course I'd just been launched six feet across the road by one of them and the other had this sawed-off shotgun, so I guessed they didn't want to shake my hand.

I took off down this one-way street, which looked like it went on forever. Seeing a dark alley of to the right side, I figured they would just run right by. Maybe I didn't realize that I had entered a *God zone* and had been given a way of escape, to accept my miracle, which seemed like the only

House of Angels

Sketch of Alley

way of entering, "*The House Of Angels*". Did I want to enter here or face the alternative--death running after me? At first, I wondered why they weren't shooting or closing in faster, with the abilities they had just demonstrated. With my panic, and prayers of total desperation, maybe this was God starting to help me. Into the dark alley I ran and, to my total surprise, it was a dead end; no exit! In just a second, which seemed like an hour, the two people who had just accosted me came round the corner of the alley. In total panic again, I had to do something, about this situation. I remembered the old gospel song I had heard one time, "*When There's No Way Out Look Up*". I looked up. Here was this old rusty fire escape on the back of this old building, hanging there, in this alley. So I figured if I jumped high enough I could grab a ladder or something that might allow me to climb to higher ground, or in this case higher *anything* seemed like it would have done. But when I jumped (it is about 8 feet from the ground) I just barely got a hold of the piece of metal and

God Sends Angels : Saved From Death

nothing moved, nothing came sliding down like a step, or anything. Just to be able to jump that high seemed like a miracle. (probably God working on my case again, no complaint, "Thank you God"), yet here I was dangling in the air about 2 feet above the ground, holding onto that rusty old bottom of the fire escape ladder on the back of an old dilapidated brick building. Along came the two guys; the one with the shotgun and the other with some kind of martial arts, or something, who had already kicked me (240 pounds) across the road. So with everything I had within me I tried to lift myself up this ladder (must have been God again because I started to lift this body up the ladder), but then just to complicate things even more, here came the martial arts guy, who jumped and grabbed the bottom of my leg. As I was dragging myself up the ladder with this fellow hanging on to my leg, I had enough strength left to use the other leg and kick (it is either him off or I was going down). Well, still overwhelmed, even though I was pleading with God for deliverance, off he went and up I climbed. To the top of the ladder, I went as fast as I could possibly climb, thinking, "Well I just kicked the lion in the head and I don't think it'll make him any more pleased." All this time I was expecting that old flimsy ladder (fire escape) to let go, tumbling down on top of the three of us, which would have been a real finish to the ordeal. Then again, mister martial arts man might have come flying up after me, or the shotgun man might have started to take target practice (it had to be God helping me). I scrambled up the ladder to a door with a window; of course, the door was locked and barred from the inside. I knocked and looked through the door, thinking, "My door to freedom," but no help, no one paid me any attention. Looking through the glass, I saw a few plainly dressed older men looking my way. I shouted, "There's guys out here and they're trying to kill me. Can you open the door and help?" No way, no help from them, they all went into their separate rooms like a hotel, and closed their doors behind them. I smashed the glass, unlocked the door, and went inside. Crunching over the broken glass, I walked as fast as I could down this long hallway, with the sound of doors slamming shut. As I journeyed on, listening for the voices or sounds of my pursuers, I saw an empty open room, done up like a hotel room, with no sign of any habitation. So I took the opportunity, slipped inside, and shut and locked the door. Standing in the dark I waited, thinking, praying, and of course having all kinds of thoughts about fear and how it was trying to eat me alive. "Am I going to be killed by these maniacs running after me, or what is really going to happen?" On and on my thoughts rambled. "Who really are these guys and why are they trying to hurt me with such intensity?" One of them looked like the guy I worked for in the teardown job I never went back to. Maybe something had gone wrong the day I never showed up, and they were somehow blaming me for it. Or maybe they were just mean and saw someone on the back streets, late at night and figured it was a good chance for target practice, (but sure going far out of the way for a kick at a single person all alone in the night).

The night before (now it was about 3 am), I remembered slipping a bit from the salvation I knew as a boy and had been drinking some. I should have known better, but it was grace—God's grace—that didn't condemn me right away. I had thought a little party, a little fun on the wild side; God won't care; I'd get away with it, no problem. So I thought now, "Look at the mess I'm in. I wonder if morning is coming again and if I'll make it in one piece or not. Dear God please help me, I am your child, I've messed up and if you help me out of this mess I'll promise never to follow these steps into this mess again. And I'll serve you with all my heart and soul."

Just as I finished my short little prayer, I heard a couple of people coming up the stairs, running, and going to the door with the broken glass, crunching, shuffling around, hammering on the doors shouting, "Has anybody seen anyone come in here?" Here I was locked in this shabby little hotel room behind a door, about the thickness of cardboard, waiting at any moment for the door to come crashing in and my pursuers to enter. I looked out the window of the room, but there was no escape, just another flat roof going nowhere. Just the three edges away from the wall of the

God Sends Angels : Saved From Death

building I was in. But God was not out of ways of providing an escape. Just a short time passed, and a very loud clear-sounding set of footsteps came from the direction of the stairs, and quickly arrived over where my pursuers were. I listened intently (similar to when I had listened in Sunday School to the Bible stories I loved), to the sound of a new player in this dilemma. Upon his arrival at the location where all the activity is taking place, I heard a very stern voice of authority asking, "Who are you and what are you doing here?" (To the two people pursuing me) and they replied that they are the police in search of this individual they thought came through the back door there. Then the single individual spoke again and said, "This is my building and in here you are nothing of the sort, so you're both going out." Just as he finished, I heard a little scuffle, and a brief pause. After a short time I heard the same footsteps that had just come up the stairs, along with another couple of sets of feet mainly just bounced along. It sounded like one individual going back down the stairs and two others being dragged or carried out and away. In quietness, I waited, listening and wrestling with the thought, "Could this saving grace have been carried out by an angel sent by God to minister salvation for His children?" In the stillness that followed, I made use of the room and fell asleep, with my mind tensed at first, and then feeling the peace that salvation brought.

    The next morning I woke up with the feeling that the birds' singing sounded so much sweeter, the sunshine was much brighter, and I had a real sense of having been given a fresh new start. The previous night of war for me definitely was over and I was still alive, thank you God. In my human reasoning, I am to this day not sure how it happened. As I opened the door that morning and walked out into the hallway, I wondered what I would see. I went on, praying all the way. The window was still smashed out, but no one was to be seen anywhere. I called out, not too loud. I would have been happy to repay someone for the pane of glass and definitely would have thanked them for the intervention in my past night of horror, but no one was in sight. I walked down the stairs, and kept on calling for someone, but still no one was in sight. What I arrived at what was like a hotel lobby with a counter and chairs along with other furniture items, nobody was in sight. As I walked away, the radio was playing a gospel song, *"Throw out the life line; throw out the life line, some one is drifting away. Throw out the life line, throw out the life line, someone is sinking today"*.

Yes Victory

It's in the valleys where the real race is run,
Knowing the eternal values of the soul are begun;
It's Jesus who brings victory over Satan's snares,
Making known to you all tested everywhere.

Though many times we've fallen so low,
There's always Jesus to whom we can go;
When Satan like a storm strives to overcome,
We can turn to the Master, God's chosen Son

I've now the roadmap to my home on high,
Waiting for Jesus coming through the sky
Where we'll live forever by his precious side,
No more life in sin, in victory to abide.

Yes, it's victory needed and victory to guide
To live with Jesus on the heavenly side,
So that this world shall find God will provide
Completing victory, where we can always abide.

Sometimes in the night or even the day
We may be tested beyond what's OK
God sent his angels their mission to save,
To rescue his children, they're always so brave.

We call for his mercy, his power and might-
Please come and deliver, help in the fight.
The enemy gets too close, defeat is all around;
Gods sends his angels, victory is found.

God Sends Angels : Narrow Bridge

Really, this whole adventure was a real assurance there really is a higher power that I believe is God and that He cares for us His children when we call on Him, and can help us. That night I went through, with the intervention by an angel, proved a night spent in a house of angels. In the morning, I walked up the street and found my way back to my apartment, packed my bags and headed down the road out of town on a bus bound for the next city, and of course for my next adventure, with the fresh knowledge, "Man! There really is a higher power and He really does care."

Narrow Bridge

There was this second real up-close encounter with angels in my life. In the Bible we read in Hebrews 1:13, 14 *"Are not all angels ministering spirits sent to serve those who will inherit salvation?"* So in prayer I'm always remembering that, even though I'm only human, God loves me enough to take care of me. Not just to teach me His ways, but also to protect me by sending a response team (His holy angels) to a critical situation. By accepting the gift of salvation at a very young age, I gained the knowledge of Him and the life-long benefits of belonging to God. At least I spent most of my life living with the promise of eternal life rising from the old body that will be sown in the ground, to a new life eternal, just like our saviour Jesus. No matter what their age, a person can still accept Him.

Well here's a real interesting story that happened one day while I was driving home to Prince Edward Island, from visiting my brother in law and sister in North Sydney, Cape Breton. That's where I had met this girl, Rose MacQueen, who was my sweet heart, to become my wife. So I had a strong reason to be there! Heading east towards the PEI ferry, just by New Glasgow back then there were several very narrow bridges over roads going in and out of the town. When I was crossing one of these bridges, I saw ahead several big heavy metal box trucks carrying coal. Just a few seconds before this I had noticed beside me, in the van I was driving, what appeared to be an angel—just there with no sound or anything—just there looking straight ahead along the road.

> ### Moving Along
> Words & music by Loman Bell recorded on the album Hopefield Sunrise
> Chorus:
> Well I'm moving along, singing my song,
> With Jesus, I know I belong.
> In day time or night, guided by the light,
> Which is Jesus, this Saviour of mine.
>
> Gliding like a boat, o'er this sea we float,
> Towards the port and our Saviour's open arms,
> No time to be still, but working until,
> The call comes to at last come home.
>
> You don't need a map; the Bible is all of that,
> Showing the way to all who are moving along.
> Feet are some times sore, but doesn't uneven the score,
> For God will have final count of all.
>
> If someone should ask, "What is the task?"
> Tell them, to bear the cross all the way.
> Jesus does know, one day He will show,
> That really your faith outweighs all the facts.

    A few seconds later, I was coming up onto these bridges, meeting these coal trucks. On the bridge, there was a walkway on one side, and just barely enough room for two-way traffic. Ahead I noticed at a glance, on the walkway a woman with children and baby carriage, and another person coming towards them on a bicycle. Just when we where almost beside them, the cyclist rode off the sidewalk, not noticing the trucks coming up behind. Once on the road, he forced the big coal truck to cross the centre line, making a front-end collision with the oncoming traffic seem inevitable. The image fresh in my mind of the angel in my van, gave me assurance that everything was going to be all right, along with the promise from God, "*Here on earth with Him or home*

God Sends Angels : Narrow Bridge

Moving Along

Moving Along At Night

in Heaven with Him." The old hymn rang loud and clear in my mind, *"Blessed assurance Jesus is mine, oh what a foretaste of glory divine."* There was absolutely no room to go apart from straight ahead, into these big coal trucks and the overwhelming collision of a hundred tons or more hitting me in a one-ton mini van. Just at that instant, it seemed like I just drove into a mist, an intervention from God. It happened again! I found myself driving out the other side of the bridge, still on the road, still in one piece still praising God and looking around at no accident, no damage, and all in one piece.

Hope

Don't let the lights go out
That burn within my heart.

Compassion, love and mercy
Always help to make a start.

When silence is the loudest,
That's when we hear the call.

Rain falling on everyone,
The just and unjust alike.

The truth becomes so evident,
On who receives our praise.

Even where life has no more trust,
To whom do we take it up?

Who'll come and help us now?
To Thee our voices raise.

All men just follow the course of destiny;
Tomorrow will come, where will we be?

Always seeing the conditions of man,
Living to experience the Master's plan,

Weaving through it, we acknowledge
Life is just a short time,

Heavenly beings around everywhere,
Unseen battle, His victory clear.

No other power can finally say,
"It's finished forever, our (God's) way".

God Sends Angels : Out From Under The Truck

Rainbow of Hope

That sure was enough of a reason to keep on believing and trusting in God's unfailing love and concern for His children. I believe He's the same yesterday, today and forever—if only we could really grasp the intense love of God we would see and feel His power to save us in many situations.

Out From Under The Truck

The third time I had an angel come to my rescue, was the most extreme that I can remember. It was at one of those times in a Christian's life when you find yourself kind of low and even slipping into all kind of things like "Is this salvation really worth all this separation?" When it seems like people who live it up don't seem to be having near as much trouble day by day. All kinds of thoughts like that spring up where you would have trouble even distinguishing between what is positive and what is negative. Where then would you turn for the answers? Is drinking or drugs or something to get you high, going to give you the way out of your time of problems, and troubles, or are you just going to drift along and maybe not even care about the future or whatever? All

House of Angels

The Homestead

these thoughts left me fighting confusion, especially in the mind. Naturally, this was a time I was out of work. We had two young children and their needs had to come first. With all these pressures, money seemed to be hard to come by.

Vehicles were always breaking down, or just broken junk. So I leaped for joy at the offer from a preacher that he would give us his old car. It needed some repairs, inspection, and a license to get it ready for the road. So we towed the vehicle to the farm and did some work—lights, wipers, and an appointment to get the inspection which would tell us what kind of shape it was underneath, brakes, etc.

At the same time, we were driving this big Bronco and for sure, it was hard on gas, at the least, compared to the car we were going to try to fix up. So the plan was, use the truck for off-road work around the farm, in the woods, for towing, and doing the heavy things cars can't do. We had a big set of mud and snow grip tires for the Bronco, which I intended to install in front of the house using the old V-shaped jack from my father's service station days.

As the story goes, I called the inspection station to get an appointment for the other car in a couple of hours. I phoned my friend and neighbour, Harry Buell, to drive me to the house after I had taken the car to the station for the inspection. Now I had a couple hours to fill, so I figured I

God Sends Angels : Out From Under The Truck

The Bronco

might as well start to change the four tires on the Bronco and put on the big ones for the winter. I put this triangle V-shaped jack under the back bumper and started to lift the truck. Of course, the truck has a 5.5-inch lift kit installed in it, and the height difference between the small tires coming off and the big tires going on is an added 6 inches. I had the jack up to the top and there still wasn't enough clearance to put the big tires on. With the smaller tires off, I figured I'd just dig a little hole under the general area where one tire was going to go. What I didn't realize was that the hole wasn't the right size for the big tire! Also the jack, at the very top of its track, has lifted the whole back end of the truck off the ground. The big problem with this was I had planned to only change *one* tire today—just a few minutes and no need for axle stands or support of any kind, like blocks, which I usually have under the frame, but not this time. Anyway, because this big tire was so heavy and awkward, I was down on my knees trying to force the tire on the axle and, a little push wasn't doing it, so I pushed and wiggled it more and more with one arm over the top of the tire and the other arm sort of across the bottom. Then it happened! A big push brought the truck off the jack and, with a *crunch*, it came down on the top of the tire with my arm caught in the middle. There I was stuck solid, chin up against the fender, on my knees, feeling this sharp pain, and starting to feel faint.

Suddenly out to the rear of the truck, by the bumper where the jack was, I saw this most amazing, beautiful person—a figure that seemed about 8 feet tall, all aglow, as bright as fire, lit up as colourful as a Christmas tree, and at that same instant, I felt the truck being lifted off my arm. The next thing I found myself *standing*, leaning against the side of the truck, holding my badly broken, mangled arm up on top of the other arm. Hallelujah! His Word says, *"He will give His angels charge over thee, lest you dash your foot against a stone"* (Psalm 91). So here I was standing against the truck, trying to walk to the house, not wanting to fall on the ground where the dog would probably lick me to death. I reached the front of the house, managed to get the door open, sort of stumbled inside, calling out to Rose, "Call an ambulance, my arm is broken." She was in the middle of making bread and thought I was joking, so she asked me, "Will you wait until I have let the yeast rise?" As I fell on my knees, almost passing out, she realized it was serious. Phoning the hospital, she reported I was passing out. They told her to have me put my head between my legs—with my size that would be impossible at any time! She asked for an ambulance but there were none available right then. Then she phoned Harry to see if he could drive me to the hospital. By an amazing "coincidence", he had the day off and was home, so he comes right over and of to the hospital we go. We went to the King's County Hospital first, but they determined a cast wasn't going to work—too serious an injury. Off to town we went. We pulled into the emergency department at the Queen Elizabeth Hospital, went inside the emergency department and I passed out, falling into the wheel chair. Then the doctor checked a heavy cast to see if it would work but to no satisfaction. The next step was an operation to install a plate in the broken arm to hold it together while the bones, which were badly mangled, healed together. The anaesthesiologist took me under to the tune of *Amazing grace how sweet the sound that saved a wretch like me, I once was lost but now...* and I was out like a light. When I came to, they confirmed that the operation was a success

God Sends Angels : Out From Under The Truck

but I still faced months of healing and therapy.

Thank you God, for the wonderful miracle—bringing me out of this serious trouble. I believe He can do it for you if you believe and ask, in Jesus name. As you walk with Him, expect at any time to look over your shoulder and see the hand of God at work, even by sending His angels to help you.

Free Free Free

Oh Lord, soften my heart, like You showed to me,
Disappointment may come here on life's stormy sea;
Friends may leave our side, yet You're always there;
We can call Your name and You always care.

It's kind of like when the angels rolled the stone away,
Jesus Christ our Saviour, arose and walked away,
The resurrection power and all authority,
Washed in the blood of the Lamb and He set us free.

We can live with Him forever,
Upon that golden shore, where angels sing and praise the
  King they adore,
When time will change forever into eternity.

My Early Years

Parents

Hello, My name is Loman Bell. I'm the younger of two children of Darrel and Agnes Bell. Born on Prince Edward Island, in Kings County, Murray River, my mother was originally Agnes MacFarlane from Hopefield and my father was Darrel Bell, originally from Abney.

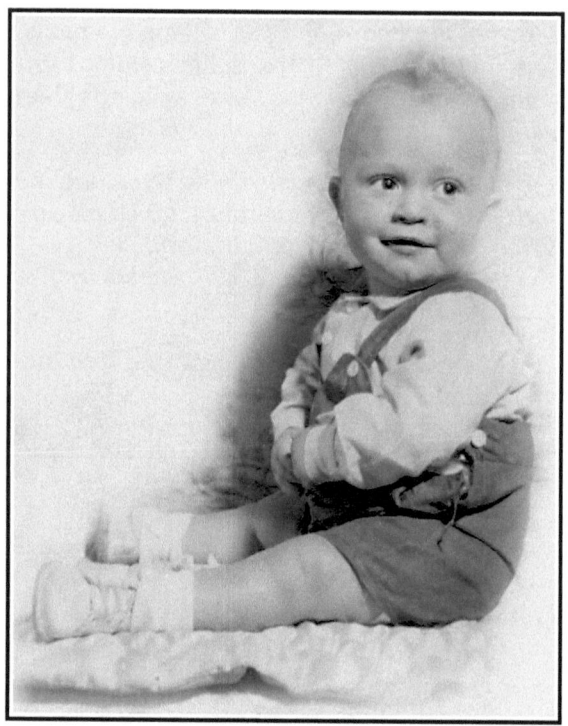

Loman Bell

Mother And Dad's Getting Together In those days mother would be at the concerts in the halls. She was about fifteen. She played the Hawaiian steel guitar and sang Christmas carols or other songs on different occasions. Dad would

My Early Years: Parents

always play along at these events with the guitar and fiddle and joining in with the groups, which gave them a perfect opportunity to be acquainted. This would be a real connecting point, where you would have a lot of fun playing and singing at the concerts, especially when this was one of the main activities in the area. Afterwards people would gather in their homes for more playing and of course, lots of good home made delights to eat. This continued with both of them playing, singing, and eventually falling in love. Then along comes the love bug. They tie the knot continuing to play and perform until after my sister and I kind of break up the party bringing on the excitement and caring of the baby years. For most of the child rearing years, mother hung up her guitar, for house chores, just playing some with dad in church functions.

My mother and father did a lot of their courting on a sleigh or horse-drawn wagon. The story goes on, that one time Dad owned a horse that used to deliver milk at each house. On their journey home in frigid temperatures, they would huddle, almost invisible under a big buffalo blanket, to drive the sleigh. The horse would lead the way, going up every lane of the milk route, all the way up and down the winding old road. These unintended visits on their way home would startle many farmers, thanks to the well-trained horse.

As a child, my mother had worked around her family home doing house chores and some farm-related duties as well. When the neighbours needed help taking in their harvest (good equipment such as tractors were rare and labour was the most needed part of harvesting), they would call on their neighbours and the youth available to work. She told of working on the potato harvest back then when they'd do most of the picking by hand. The old beater diggers, drawn by horse or tractor, would beat the potatoes out into the drill between the rows of potatoes. Then the labourers would come with baskets picking up the potatoes, which sometimes would mean also grading them, and carry the baskets to the wagons where they would stay either in the baskets or whatever holding area they would have for them. Even on the farm that we now call home, my mother would stay overnight and work at harvest time. The school she attended is still partially standing, across the road from where we now live—just a little country, one-room schoolhouse—yet at one time it was a bustling centre of activity for the neighbourhood.

Early House

As a boy, father had helped farm and had many other jobs that were available at that time. He'd go into the fields early mornings with a horse and plough, sometimes bare footed through the fields, clearing ground, moving rocks and stumps, or whatever else had to be done. Dawn until dusk—it was a hard day's work—with usually the only reward being comfort in knowing your work was being done and getting a bite to eat, even if it only was potatoes. There were always the chores to do around the animals, with their cleaning, feeding, making their beds in the barns, stalls, or wherever they would bed down for the night. On and on it went. He would work off the farm if he could for a buck or two. He along with others in the community would load

My Early Years: Horses

freight cars with potatoes, etc., for the railroad, at the loading ramps such as the one in Murray River, just behind where the Murray River Library is now located.

Home to the farm, all of the work waiting for them, depending on who was around to share the chores and help with the work. While he was growing up there, my father was also one of the main people to fire up the old pot-bellied stove to heat the Abney's one room schoolhouse.

Younger Years

I loved going along on the drag sleigh. I enjoyed being around the daily farm life and have always respected the hard work of my dad and the example he set for me. "Always try to survive, son, no matter how hard the job may be, keep your hand to the plough."

Horses

In those years we drew our water from the brook beside the home farm, down over the hill, through the field. Sometimes I rode along on the drag sleigh, I can still see the horse's breath on a cool crisp fall or winter day as it hauled that drag sleigh and a barrel from the brook. You could hear the squeaking and crackling sound of the sleigh as it moved along. The horse would always give its response to pulling the load with a snort or a wheee! The horse was such a good animal to have around. On the farm, it was worth its weight in gold, for working. Then also, there were those times when the sleigh was travelling empty. We had a little time to have some fun, so jumping on and off; through the fields we'd go, the horse enjoying its run, the snow flying, the nice crisp, cool, fresh air blowing in your face, the crunching of the snow, as we would tag along on the sleigh ride.

Hopefield Farmer
words and music by Loman Bell also on Hopefield Sunrise album.
Up with the sun, working away,
Driving the mail, on his way,
Cows to milk, chores to be done,
All the way, till setting sun.

Chorus
Just a Hopefield farmer, hoping for rain,
To water the ground, help grow the grain,
Then he'll plough the field, and start again,
Another year to plant, harvest and gain.

Trying to get by, bills to pay,
Not too much money, bailing hay.
Work in the woods, hard days task,
Drive the mail if my car will last.

Time goes by, everybody knows,
Sometimes it's fast, sometimes it's slow,
God made us all, to see Him one day;
Then we'll plough the field till judgement day.

Even when it came time to put Joe, the horse, back in his nice warm stall for a bit of a break, I'd love the smell of the horse barns. Sometimes I had the job of pouring a bucket of fresh water, giving them an armful of fresh crispy

My Early Years: Horses

hay and a real good brush down and wipe to get the sweat off them. You could always see in the faces of my father and his brothers how they appreciated their animals by the way they took care of them, showing respect for them. You could almost hear the horses talking to you with the nod of their heads and the different sounds they made when you gave them attention and showed them kindness, with the things you did for them, the feeding and cleaning, trying to keep them healthy and happy. They would be trying to say thank you! Thank you! It was always so amazing seeing these massive animals running and jumping, enjoying their freedom racing through the fields. Yet they were coming right up to you so you could pet them, feeding them out of your hand with a bunch of hay or grass. Later on in life, I went on many sleigh rides with church groups. I still hear the vivid details of the crisp winter's night, hearing the crunch and crackle of the sleigh laden with fun seekers, as it would slide over the well- frozen snow. You could hear the horse snorting with sheer delight as he pulled along the load of people. Sometimes we would be singing songs with the jingle of the horses' bells as they pranced along. This would be especially nice at Christmas time with the singing of Christmas carols.

    I remember going along with my mother on some of the daily working activities like the blueberry picking. There were times when they'd be lucky to be paid a nickel a pound. At other times, I remember playing around the fish plant while my mother was putting in a day's work, and Dad was over at the bluff fishing lobster, in the Murray Harbour North area.

    When my father went fishing over on Pictou Island while still living at home in Abney. They would rise early, carrying what they would need for the trip, and trek the mile or two across the back fields and woods over to the shore at High Bank where they would load it in their dory and row over to Pictou Island, about nine miles. Over there they had a shack where they would stay sometimes a day or more. This was always depending on the weather, the time of the year, because harvest time would need all hands on deck at the farm. Sometimes they would salt fish for eating and personal

Dory Launching Spot

use, while other times they would sell some of their catches. A lot of the times as things progressed they would acquire horses and wagons for helping in the transportation, and then eventually trucks.

So then when the time was right, depending on the weather and farm work, harvesting etc., they would make the trip back to PEI, rowing and lugging their catches, Storing and taking some of their catch home for food. They would always have the salting barrels around to preserve their catches and drying fish was a common sight to see.

Growing Up

My sister and I were both reared with respect for hard work and life. We must have inherited musical ability as well. The area of our childhood (Southern King's County, PEI) was a family-oriented area, with a sort of extended family including relatives and neighbours alike. These were the days of birth and growing, in this wonderful little village of

My Early Years: Growing Up

Murray River, with my mom, dad and sister. As children, we would always have friends around or at least close by.

Loading Area For Freight Cars (Murray River)

In this community there were lumber mills sawing continually, shingle mills going full speed, the starch factories, and many other ventures in the farming, fishing, and local industries. The local shipping docks, and the local train-station loading platforms kept the exporting and receiving market going constantly.

The train stopped there in the Murray River area back around the early years of the nineteen hundreds. There were a lot of businesses, stores, a restaurant, a garage, a hotel right beside the train depot, also visitors coming and going as passengers on the train.

Also in the area, probably because it was quite a sheltered river, there would be planes landing with people on tours, and also delivering certain products.

When I was a boy, they were building a new Murray River bridge. In those days, it wasn't a common practice to put up a lot of fences or guards to stop people from walking around the construction zones. There were just traffic detours. So it was a common thing as kids, that we would

House of Angels

Loading Docks

Plane Traffic!

play around the area--even walking out on the beams that were joining the banks. Up and down both sides of the river, we'd float a boat, swim, and dig in the clay for the fun of it, as children, in those growing days, just enjoying life.

We would swim around the bridge and the joining river-

My Early Years: Growing Up

An Old Murray River Bridge

banks, jumping off the bridge. Funny as it sounds, the biggest fun we'd have would be with an old tire and a stick. We'd just roll the tire around, keeping it rolling with the stick by beating the top of the tire. Also we had lots of other home-made toys such as stilts, wooden boats, holes in the dirt where we'd play with our toy army trucks, digging, having fun. Then there was always the trip to the candy store to pick up a little treat and then push the little cart up the hill to our driveway, parking there on the sidewalk, and watching the traffic. Sometimes there would be truck traffic, hauling loads of gravel, fill, shale, or dirt of some kind, going to a road job. We would try raising our arms as kids pretending to haul down a horn, like a train whistle. A lot of times we would get a response and we'd hear this big *brmpppp!!!!* Having these truckers in these big machines taking time to pay attention to us, was exciting for us kids. My little cart was like a mobile home in a way, because I'd always have something in it, like my favourite blanket for a lay-down out in the sun, or whatever I expected I might use on my journeys. Sometimes I would drive my tricycle and tow the carts just having kid fun.

House of Angels

Early Murray River

Lots of Snow

My Early Years: Winters

Winters

In the wintertime back then the snow banks would usually be to the top of the cars and over them, burying pretty near everything in the path of these big blizzards. The roads would be blocked (early 50's) for a while, and we would walk over to the post office to get the mail, after supper, when the Harbour Train would come in. You could always hear that old familiar sound of the train whistle, and you would know it was mail time. Picking mail up at the post office was such a nice evening activity. It seemed like half the community would come out. It provided a real fun time, a break from the homework, and the daily chores just before settling in for a long winter's night. Some people were shouting and squealing. Many times you'd see people, walking, sleighing, or however, over to the post office to get their mail.

Mom and Me

Some would use the horse and sleighs for means of transportation and even taking the kids to school, just like the winter express, picking up and dropping off. Many times we'd run and hitch a ride to school; then there was no busing the children to school just walk, or whatever means of travel you could get.

Skiing In the winter, sometimes we'd have a pair of skis. So anyway, this first time I got a new pair (only about five years old) I went running quickly to the top of this hill in our back yard, which was only about 30 feet high with a gentle slope. So here I was at the top—my first experience with the down the hill skiing. I put my feet into the bindings and fastened them on, can't remember who in the family was there; I think it might have been Mom, and she sure wasn't a skier either. Anyway here I was and ready for the downhill event. Up on my feet, pole in both hands for the gentle push off, and away I go, but then to my horror straight ahead, I see the clothesline! Whoops! Forgot to check that out; too late, let out a yell and at the same instant my mouth hit the clothesline, Oww! the skis and poles went one way, and I went the other, So very sore, I climbed out of the downhill fetch up and through the snow dragged myself back up the hill to the house pretty well without any ski supplies with me. Wheee! Or I mean OWWW! So I ended my first unsupervised, at least non-experienced supervised skiing attempt. The hill was still great for down hill sliding on an old inner tube, sleighs, or whatever. Around the same time, my dad started working at the airplanes in the Charlottetown Air Force hangers and would be throwing out these old worn airplane tire tubes, so I asked for one and home he came one day with this airplane tube. When you put the air in, it got five times the size of a normal car tire. Wow! Flying down the hill with lots of rubber around gave you a sense of security, being able just to bounce off things. Later on I would attempt skiing again, only this time, it was cross-country, and I liked it better. These airplane tubes were really fun also in the water, but the wind was a real danger since it could blow you out into the channel and deep water, so we were encouraged to use a lot of caution.

Skating As kids, we had lots of fun things to do—sports, such as, skating, sliding, snow-fort building, and skiing.

My Early Years: Too Young to Chop Trees

Early Winters

Some times, we would build these wooden frames, putting skates to the bottom and then a little sail, on the frozen river, and away we'd fly—sometimes too fast and too close to the open water so it was discouraged. There was this one pond back in Abney around the old Bell, Richards, Buell, farms, where we as a family, when all the water was well frozen, would love to go. Dad would drive his old 50/51 Ford car there through the frozen fields using it as a place for changing skates and transportation as well as a power source. He'd hook up an old headlight to the battery and presto—light for our little skating rink. Those old flat head Fords in the fifties seemed to have the traction of a little tractor. So with weight in the trunk and a good set of winter tires we would be able to handle driving through the field with very little resistance.

Too Young to Chop Trees

As an adventuresome lad, I loved new challenges. One day I got hold of this little hatchet, jumped in my cart, and away I went up the hill, through the neighbours' back yard on our well-worn path through the field, Behind the houses. The path went behind where the old barbershop used to be, to my cousin's, I believe it was my cousin Basil's, where we became lumberjacks and were going to cut down a tree—around 5 years of age, we sure weren't! Here was this big beautiful white birch tree which seemed to be a good place to start. One big wind-up, the swing, and the bounce, off the tree, and into my knee goes the hatchet with a thud. There was blood everywhere, dispersing into my clothes. Not sure what to do I started home. I sat in my little cart and rolled on down the hill to our back yard where I sat in my cart, bleeding I guess until it clotted, or else probably I would have bled out. When my mother came home to find me a little while later, there I was with clothes from the knee down soaked with blood and everything else in the cart. Thank God, for a helping hand. I have always believed angels do help children too.

Sometimes I would dream and it seemed I was flying with the angels. Even though we weren't well of and not living in the richest place in the country, still it is definitely true that this God really cared about even me." He would give His angels charge over thee, lest thou dash thy foot against a stone" (Psalms 91). Even sometimes when we don't realize it God cares and can still intervene through His awesome power in a person's life weaving back and forth, helping, protecting, and delivering.

Bike Excitement

One real nice sunny Saturday afternoon, in the spring, I was riding with my dad to Charlottetown. At the little Market Square across the street from the old Holman's department store, we stopped and had a rest. Holman's store was one of the biggest stores in Charlottetown.

My dad had plans. Inside the Holman's store was a second-hand store where all kinds of things were sold. I was just busting into the age of wanting more mobility—moving around in trikes, carts, and on the water in boats, rafts. So

My Early Years: Bike Excitement

Me and a Ferry Boat Ride at Wood Islands

you can just imagine the excitement when across the street, here comes my dad with this most beautiful little 14" CCM bike. Only seven years old and now having my own special means of transportation! Wow! This faster means of transportation could mean all kinds of things, more places to go and people to see. Great move Dad, thanks; you sure know how to make a kid happy. Even this most kind, gentle man who taught me Wildwood Flower on the guitar took me on the lobster boat; we went fishing and so much more, now handing out this special little piece of a child's travelling capabilities. Wow! What a day this was proving to be—a lot of adventure for a six-year old child.

It was not the same, a few years later, when at 16, he handed me the keys to the car, saying, "Take care of it." Or even better, when he and Mother got me my very first little car—only second hand, but sure a real surprise, a little *Simca*, a four door compact, yet real transportation.

House of Angels

Me and a Friend

Halloween Every Halloween brought the terror of looking out the kitchen window and seeing the Murray River bridge all ablaze with old burning cars. Some of the rascals would push cars up out of Gormely's garage and set them on fire. Of course, this would bring the Mounties, the firemen, and any of the local help they could get. There was the Old Dam Road open, or back up accessibility through Iris where they could drive in case of emergency. There were the cars blazing away with oil and tires, and even gas in some of them burning and exploding on the bridge. At first, the bridge was constructed mainly of wood, so the big fear was it burning down. Still the firemen and volunteers managed most of the time to keep it from spreading. They would pull the old cars of the bridge and separate them so they would burn themselves out.

Water Fun

One of my cousins and I both had lobster-fishing dads so we'd hang out at the bluff down Murray Harbour North, where they fished. I remember many times going with my dad to work at the Lobstering and go with them into the cookhouse building where they'd be serving up fresh breakfast—eggs, pancakes, French toast, toast, bacon, sausage, juice, tea, coffee, and just about anything your heart

My Early Years: Water Fun

desired. Back then, in the 1950s, the water seemed a little warmer and summer sometimes came a little earlier. In June my cousin Ronnie who just lived up the road and I would get together swimming, rowing dories around. Most of all we had a real neat little raft we made ourselves and would have fun with it in the swamp. Swimming seemed to come naturally so there didn't seem to be any danger, even though we usually played alone, real captains and pirates. Also in those days, another sailing partner was my cousin Basil, who also went on later to be a real captain, in the fisheries.

Birthday Party

Water Skiing Adventure I went to the beach with friends for an afternoon of water fun one time in Nova Scotia, They had this raft out twenty to thirty feet from the shore to which we'd swim and jump off. We would also launch from the raft for a new sport they called water skiing. Eventually the good swimmers all had many turns and the boater asked if anyone else wanted to try. I was up for trying it, so with much hesitation, yet just bouncing with curiosity, I yelled out, "I'll try." I grabbed the rope from the boat, put the skis on and here I went on this great new learning experience. Or so I expected it to be. Skis on, rope tight, boat revved up, popped it into gear and we're off. Just then I realized I didn't know how to do this. I couldn't get the skis up and before I could let go of the rope, the boat had dragged me ten to fifteen feet out into deeper water. So there I was, way over my head in water, must have swallowed a gallon before when I yelled, Whoaaaaaaaaaaaa! -trying to get these confounded skies off, trying to breathe, half full of water, couldn't yell for help either, seeing my life flash before me I prayed a little and knowing God loves us, felt the strength to swim back to the raft coughing and saying, "God help me." So He did. At the raft I must have gasped, coughed, and spit up water for half an hour, then finally, when my strength came back, I swam ashore. That ended my experience with water skiing.

Murray River Ships

There was a rich ship- building community around the area. Back in the early nineteen hundreds, they built boats for fishing, freight carrying, moving goods around, and dropping imports off at the wharves, transporting people, and general travel. I remember that there was this one big sailing ship that had grounded long before just below our back yard where we used to swim and play as children (I later found out it was one of Munn's or White's boats).

So close, it made us all want to be sailor-captains. We'd climb on the decks, pretending it was sailing—to exotic places, other islands, other lands, and then, home again. At age six or seven, playing on this old ship didn't inspire any thoughts about time gone by—about the hard jobs of cutting down the trees, sawing up the planks, preparing of the materials for the shipbuilding. Nor even thoughts about this

My Early Years: Murray River Ships

Abandoned to Decay

particular ship stuck in the mud. Imagine if it could tell of the storms it may have faced, the squeaking of the timber as the ship was twisted in a cold Atlantic gale while the crew prayed for mercy and the wind blew them o'er the sea! Think about the heavy cargo nearly bringing the ship to the water line, while the waves washed on board and chilled the sailors to the bone. To us it was just a toy stuck in this mussel bed with half the hull beneath the mud.

On a crisp fall morning, you could see these hardy men off to the woods to cut wood for a ship. With their crosscut saws, axes, lunch, and water they would go into the woods, getting a big bonfire going, a kettle of water boiling, and the usual start up activities. Besides the horses, men needed brute strength to work at this, with the cutting, junking hauling out, and going off to the mill. The mill would take the wood saw it into proper pieces, and dry it. Then the ship

House of Angels

Shipping Traffic

builders would plane, saw, chisel, hammer, and start assembling this ship. After the building came filling cracks, caulking, cosmetic things, then adding the steering, and the rudders. Eventually beautiful tall masts would be draped with well-sewed sails and ties—ready for the old north wind to come blasting through the sky, testing their fabric and strength. Then down to the slip where this new ship would be added to the fleet, and would make its first big debut Into the water and watch it float, taking it for a ride around the block, well I should say up and down the channel. Then back to its mooring and checking time for any last details, for tightness etc., and ready for the load, and ship ahoy. Next stop may be Barbados or somewhere in Newfoundland exchanging Prince Edward Island potatoes or other products for meats, or fruit, nails or metals, and other needed items. So hoist the main sail, draw the anchor, chart the course, and a prayer for good weather and journeying mercies.

Then one day in the future, this fine ship would come sailing back into the river, and at high tide, they would run it aground. Putting a portable slip under for inspection at low tide, they waited. Then the inspection of the hull, with the bad news that the wood's rotten, and it needs a lot of repair. Too old and too expensive to repair, the proud ship was left to decay in the mussel sludge just where it last sailed. History notwithstanding, it sure was a nice place for us budding sailors to play, searching for bounty in the waters of our imagination.

My Early Years: Job Displacement

Job Displacement

Later on when the fishing wasn't proving out, too much hard work, too little pay, my father's love for mechanics took over. From the garage in Murray River, right next to the park there, now, across from the bank, I believe it was Johnston Garage, where they also sold cars. I used to love going there as a child after school, playing around the sawmill on the pile of sawdust, and dropping in to see Dad, who always had a big box of these nice little crackers. He worked there for a while, but there were more opportunities in Charlottetown for a very good, top-notch mechanic, so off we went, moving to the big city

Move To Town The year was around 1958. He sold his fishing fleet, chose to stay a mechanic, and applied for a job in Charlottetown, at a garage called Stewart Motors, working on the cars and vehicles brought in there for repair and whatever was needed. This gave him an opportunity to buy his very first new car, a 1966 *Meteor Rideau*, four-door, and what a beautiful car it was. Even before this, he was working at the airplanes in Charlottetown at the airport hangers, in repairs and maintenance, replacing the gauges and trouble-shooting.

Later he applied to Texaco service stations for a leasing agreement. After a training session in Texaco's school for operators, he took over the station at 222 Queen Street, Charlottetown, home of Bell's Texaco until around 1970.

The accident he was in some twenty years earlier left him with very bad hips. Because of this injury, (a broken hip) back in the 1940s, where he and a few buddies were driving out from town, and a few of them had too much to drink, heading towards Cherry Valley corner, too fast, wrong combination. So when dad saw the corner coming up, he lunged ahead getting stuck in between the two bucket seats, trying to turn the keys of and stop the car. This corner was nearly a ninety- degree corner, and at sixty or seventy miles an hour, the car rolled over and over quite a few times, snapping his hip quite badly, leaving him in a body cast for most of a year. So then in service station work, this thirty

House of Angels

years later, with some more operations needed to give him mobility with less pain, he had to consider the type of work.

With all the running around, and lease agreements going sky high, he decided to try other things, other jobs, even schooling, like courses in plumbing and heating. He bought a few big apartment houses and did room-and-board for a while. He bought and built cottages in Brackley for the tourist business. At one time Mother tried working at Kirkwood Motel as night check in, baking and shipping goods to the stores for sale, and as a seamstress. Always through all these years, the main thing I can remember was their attempt to survive no matter what and provide for their children the best they could. Through all these times, there was always a desire to put God first and keep faith in the home.

Years before this, back around the early 1930s Dad also, with the family in tow, moved to the town of Mongell, Quebec, where he worked at the Air Force hangers, fixing and troubleshooting the big carriers and bombers, etc. That was a real neat experience, growing up with the French-speaking kids and learning the language fluently. It was a real nice time in my life, when we spent a Christmas in the area and had a party at the Air Force hangers where they spared no expense for their staff and their family and friends. The airport hangers must have covered ten acres, and every part of it had fun and games, and lots to eat. Coming back from all those journeys, gave me memories I could never forget. All the friends and people who just wanted to get to know you was such an adventure in the kindness of people in general. Also this was after the main part of World War Two, with a treaty being signed between the warring factions. This brought a real vivid sense of relief and celebration. Though with respect for the tremendous price paid by our fallen country's soldiers. We were in a state of victory because of them.

Stuck in a Snow Bank After his contract was over in Quebec in the Air Force, we headed home. There we still had a house and land in the village of Murray River. On the trip home, in the dead of winter, snow-covered roads, in an old

My Early Years: Church Influences

Ford panel truck, the heater barely working, yet journeying on, there was barely any room in this one-seat truck, since we had to throw away the other seats for carrying room. My sister and I ended up on the very top of everything in the back of the truck on our mattress, just lying there for the journey that must have taken almost a day's travelling. At one place here on the Island we hit a snowstorm and eventually hit a snow bank that stopped us completely. Even after Dad tried to shovel us out, there was no way out until the snow ploughs would be back on the roads in the morning. The area was just around the hills, in the Bonshaw area, around Strathgartney park. I believe it was the highest point on Prince Edward Island. Thank God, during the storm a very kind neighbour came to the truck where we were snowed in, snow up to the windows, and not very much heat, in one of the Island's good old-fashioned winter blizzards. The man took us to his home where they gave us hot drinks and food, with a place to stay until we got our old truck back on the road. For most of the trip, we drove on a wing and a prayer with our hope in Dad to take us safely home. Finally after a comforting night at this kind neighbour's house, we were on our way again, and so off we went home sweet home building a world of memories.

Church Influences

Early Years As a baby, and as long as we lived in the area, I was part of the local church. Around age seven, I had the amazing grace experience. Those early years of going to church, reading the Bible, hearing the preaching, and singing the old songs of the faith were learning years for me. We had fellowship with people of all ages—especially at first in the little church in Murray River around 60 years ago. Since I had a Bible as a young child, I would leaf through it even when I could only look at the pictures Those pictures started my curiosity about angels. Then too, I would hear the preachers telling angel stories, like the one where Jacob wrestled with the angel all night, wouldn't let him go, and ended up with a hip out of joint for life.

> **This Precious Jesus**
>
> When despair may grip your heart, turn to Jesus.
> Too many cares tear us apart, turn to Jesus.
>
> Sickness and pain, striving in vain, only Jesus;
> The Son of God, the Lamb was slain, turn to Jesus.
>
> Turn to Jesus, he's the King of Kings forever.
> He can heal your body, mind and soul.
>
> Turn to Jesus, the sweetest Rose of Sharon,
> The Lily of the Valley, the Bright and Morning Star.
>
> In this world, doubts may come, and many questions,
> How people can be so cruel and mean,
>
> What they need is to plead in the name of Jesus;
> Confess your sin, He'll take you in, His name is Jesus.
>
> Some day soon, through the clouds we'll look and see His
>   coming;
> The bride of Christ will meet Him in the air.
>
> And forever more we'll live in that home with Jesus,
> Walk streets of gold, with saints of old, and our precious
>   Jesus.

Mother was one of the first people in the Murray River Pentecostal Church, back in the years when the group was first forming. Some of the beginning preachers included the Meyer family and the Reid family. Also singers like the Libby Band, who came in this great big bus, and of course many local singers and musicians. So when we had church, a lot of the times, especially Sundays, I'd find myself being taken along to the meeting with Mother and Dad, even in my youngest years. In those days, we'd have a lot of home meetings—probably the start-up group that formed the church back in the 1940s. It sure was nice going to the homes like

My Early Years: Old Fashioned Church

the Richard family farm down in Abney or the Moore family home on the Commercial Road going to Montague, near the goose sanctuary is, and many others. There we would have Bible study, prayer, and of course a real nice lunch, and good old -fashioned fellowship. Back then of course, we used the King James Version of the Bible. There weren't other translations around very much in the early fifties that I can remember anyway. The Bible played a big role in our lives, with the reading, memorization, studying, and so on. In the early years, the reading of these Scriptures with such passion would make them sound, when coming from the elders, as though they just got them fresh from God. Hallelujah! It became such an extremely important time in my life—so interesting at just five years old to hear and see these saints of God have such enthusiasm. At the same time, we the children would hear and learn how to pray, usually on our knees. Everybody would pray on their knees out of desire and respect because we were addressing almighty God in person, coming before the Throne. I still remember with sincerity these times of following and learning because I now see how it was preparing me for the road ahead, with this pathway weaving through my life in so many extreme directions, yet still home. It is still my desire today to keep this passion alive for God's sake and for necessity.

Old Fashioned Church

Singing Just an old-fashioned church where the people were all in one accord, especially once they had an encounter with the saving grace of God. As a very young child, it stuck in my mind that the singing seemed so loud you could hear everybody like a great big choir getting ready for a performance, and now I realize yes that's right, they were. Of course the performance was singing from your heart for Jesus when everybody would act as if He was right there participating too. Those songs would continue to ring through my mind all my life, sometimes even into the next day, and the next, and what a joyful experience that was. The wonderful old hymns, like; Amazing Grace; The Old

House of Angels

Early Church Photo

Rugged Cross; Throw Out The Life Line; Shall We Gather At The River; and so many, many more you could sing forever and hallelujah that's right we will, around the throne of God. While I remember what I can, I wish there had been video cameras around then to record all those moments, which I cherish with all my heart. Sitting on the seat or lying down trying to sleep, I could feel the floor vibrating with the excitement, as the songs would begin. There were the deep base voices of the hard-working men praising God from their hearts full of gratitude for Him taking them through another trying day—a day out in the fields and barns, farming the rough old ground, breaking the sod for survival of their families, now here in church praising God for His blessings. There were also the voices of the women with the altos and heart-felt praises to God for the many blessings they had. Though they'd had only basics in life, like the making the bread totally by hand, baking it in a wood stove even in the heat of the summer, yet here together blending their voices,

My Early Years: Old Fashioned Church

and it would make the rafters ring. Singing together you could see and hear the children as soon as they would try, moving along with the beat of the songs and joining in with this heavenly choir; to me it pretty well sounded like the voices of angels! Sometimes the clapping would nearly deafen you, yet it would resemble a form of worship, "Clap your hands all you people," so it seemed to come from God, blessing you with peace and assurance that there really was a God and that He really cared. Also sometimes there was special ministering in song where people or groups would sing their heartfelt praises to God.

Running the Race
words & music by Loman Bell;recorded on the album Hopefield Sunrise.

When this race that I run, has been over and done
I'll stand before the Master that day
And hear His "Well done, my child, welcome home,
You've run the race and finished ok!"

Chorus:
Are you running the race, for the prize of His grace?
Where will you stand on that judgement day?
With all sin washed away, no more time for delay,
God will greet you along that golden way.

There've been tests everyday, along this pilgrim way,
Jesus was there through everyone,
Storms toss and sway, Jesus whispers ok!
Soon your race will be finished and won.

Now there're troubles everywhere, news of worry and care,
Still the Master whispers, "peace be still."
All men still need Him, to save us all from sin,
Guide us triumphant, to our mansion on the hill.

Testimonies In every service, the time always came for testimonies, and that just seemed to set people free. Well you could almost think these precious saints of God were jumping up for a thousand dollars or something, with the first one up would win the prize, because as soon as the song leader or preacher would say, "Is there anybody who would have anything to thank God for tonight?" the whole service would take on this new awakening. Two or three would jump to their feet at the same time but even though they were just bursting to say what they wanted to say, they would excuse themselves and courteously give each other the," you go first". It would always be in an orderly fashion of excitement and praise. Then we'd hear the shouts of joy from most, praising God. They would thank Him for the day, thank Him for life, protection, taking them through sickness, or delivering them from it, for the animals that were sick and survived, the provisions, the providence, the love of God and His saving grace. So much more, time wouldn't allow you all the time it would take to tell everything. You would have just had to be there to see all the excitement. Of course as children, we would enjoy these precious people, and even sometimes, you would hear chuckles from the listeners when some would speak because they might be lacking in some areas of education, like spelling or even pronunciation. Still they would speak in such adoration of God; you couldn't help but know that maybe these people too might have been through an encounter with angels, like Jacob. So of course as children we grew to speaking in public too, we would look for an opportunity to talk about our experiences in life. Especially when we'd experienced the new birth and knowing this God who made all the earth would actually send His Son, who willingly came and died on the cross for man; how can you turn your back on someone who loves and cares for us like that? This would give us the same desire to take a stand, proclaiming, "Praise God, He set me free too." So I started off my journey believing and expecting God to be there everyday for me to. Sometimes I wonder if the more educated we've become the more, we've lost some of the sincerity (I don't want to knock education—it has brought us some real good things). Well anyway, back to this praising church service where you could feel the love growing on you with the singing, the testimonies from people who just

My Early Years: Old Fashioned Church

wanted help in life, and found it in God.

> ### Jesus My Friend
> *I'm going to praise His name, for He is my Friend,*
> *Once I was lonesome, in need of a friend;*
> *Once my heavy burden seemed like it would never end;*
> *Once my heart was heavy burdened so low,*
> *Once bound by sin, but sin had to go.*
>
> *I've found a Friend named Jesus,*
> *I've found a true friend in Him.*
> *He took my sin and strife*
> *And gave eternal life in heaven;*
> *I found a real friend in Him.*
>
> *On the road that's winding through life with many snares,*
> *You may sometimes be caught unawares;*
> *Just put your trust in Him; then you can depend,*
> *With His precious love He'll be there till the end.*
>
> *I now see the portals and the Saviour's open arms,*
> *These arms that kept and guarded from all the Devil's harms,*
> *I know He is able to keep until the end,*
> *When at last we'll look face to face at our dearest friend.*
>
> *Still there are so many who do not know the Lord,*
> *Walking sin's pathway carrying a heavy load;*
> *Oh why not turn to Jesus? then you will find*
> *The reason God sent Him to save all mankind.*

Offering Then people looked for other opportunities to thank God for what He has done for them. We'd take up an offering and pass the plate, a hat, or a dish around and give unto the Lord. Back then a lot of people wouldn't have any money most of the year until harvest time, or when the catch was in, so money could be very scarce. I remember the salary even for the preachers could be very small and sometimes nothing, except the members of the congregation would be more than willing to share the produce from their hand's work, on the land or in the sea. So you could see the plate passed around sometimes very scarce of cash, yet you would still hear the thanks for it and with just as much of what I've come to know as faith. God will provide! Praise God and thanks. If you could hear all the praise from the early preachers, you would hear them saying they were down to their last crust of bread, without food even for special diet. Then out of the blue came a knock at the door and provisions were left on the doorstep.

Preaching Usually then came the time in the service when the man or woman of God would have an opportunity to break the Bread of Life, as sometimes they would call the sermon or the message. So with no amount of introduction, usually the time would be right for this part of the service. Always the Holy Bible would be the book for references; the reading of God's Word, with much fervour and praise, preaching time would begin. Some of these preachers would almost wake the dead with a good loud voice. There was sure no need of microphones, and a lot of shouting in response. The jubilant victory of God's promises like, "Don't give up. God loves you. He'll help you make it through all the way to our heavenly home above." Most of the time the people would respond to the preaching with a shout of praise and in agreement with the message the preacher was giving. There were preacher's who would run up and down the isles with the power of God radiating from them, with such amazing results, you couldn't help but know there was really something to serving God this way. I've seen some of the early preachers get so blessed they would jump high enough to land on the pulpit, or over the seats. They would always keep everything decent and in order, and according to Scripture. The dancing in the Spirit, and the clapping of hands, the wave offering, shouting of praises, were all encouraged in a form of worship to almighty God. In the Pentecostal circles they would always seek the infilling of the Holy Spirit, with the signs following, the gifts of the Spirit like tongues, tongues and interpretation, prophesying, all the loving kind

My Early Years: Evangelistic Rallies

infilling of the Holy Spirit would bring. Always the entire Word of God was respected and followed in every way that was understood.

Altar Call Perhaps thirty or forty minutes later, the time would come for an altar call where people would have an opportunity to get saved—this born again experience, that I believe all Christians must go through, just by believing in Jesus, God's Son, and asking Him to come into your heart, confessing you believe that, God raised Him from the dead. Also the altar time would give other Christians the time to participate in helping with people by loving them and praying for them with the preacher's encouragement. As well, this time of the service would be a good opportunity for people with special needs like sickness and infirmities, when the body of believers would agree together and pray. So to end of the service usually people would just play the instruments, singing, praising God, shaking hands, greeting one another. Then you went home with the assurance that you were in the presence of Jehovah, knowing there were holy angels all around everywhere.

Evangelistic Rallies

In Murray River around the early 1940's there was a group called the MacDonalites—a group of people who had fervency for God. They wanted His visitation and presence in their services. In this church building, close to where the Murray River library is today, in their evening service, the people would respond to the presence of God moving—they called it getting the works. When the service time would begin, also involving the Sacrament, the people would be having church, and then came time for the passing out of the bread and the wine. As each was received, you would see the people responding in strange ways like shouting, jumping up raising their hands, the women's hats sometimes would go flying off, and other exciting times, so I'm told. I imagine that the power of God was so real, people just wanted to get closer to Him. So God would answer the earnest seeking of His people and let His presence be real. At this same time, it was a great place for spectators too—they would park outside on the grass and on the road in their horse and carts and watching with great curiosity all the activity going on inside. Many people believe this was one of the first ways that evangelism started moving in the area.

The Ransom Paid

Born to die, I wonder why,
My Saviour came down to earth;
Then I knew deep inside, why for me Jesus died,
The ransom price for the sin was paid,

Not with silver, nor with gold,
With His blood, I am made whole;
Here where only sin had trod, now lives the love of God,
The ransom paid for all my sin.

If time could tell, I'd know so well,
God's plan in everything to come,
Especially in His Son who was sent God's only One;
He was the ransom paid for all my sin.

He was the ransom that was paid, yes, they placed Him in a tomb;
Praise God He arose again.
Now He lives on high, in our home, the sweet bye and bye;
He was the ransom for all the sins of mankind.

At the same time, there was a group of believers having prayer meetings in the craft shop building beside where Murray River Pentecostal Church is now—a place called Horton's Hall. This place too was filled with people who were earnestly seeking God and His power. It drew in many people from the communities including my mother, who had her born-again experience there. That group later started a church there, called Glad Tidings. They met in an old renovated barn that may have been hauled there with the Richards men and others doing the hauling and others doing renovating including my Dad. This original church burned

My Early Years: Evangelistic Rallies

down in the late 1960s when Fred Day was the pastor. They say it was because of the pot-bellied stove—it got too much fire in it and exploded. Another big project—the people got together under Clyde Slaunwhite and built the present church building in only five days. Wheeeuuu! That's good timing. The old parsonage, that was recently demolished, was hauled up the Murray River on the ice in the early 1950s. Through many of these building efforts, the workers were being fed at our house with my mother's great cooking giving them an opportunity to get to know each other better.

> ### Giving Thanks
> *When you wake up in the morning, take a little time,*
> *Thank God for making this world yours and mine.*
> *Then do your chores, for the Lord and your fellow man,*
> *And when your life is over, you've done the best you can.*
>
> *In this life we're living here, sometimes there's troubles;*
> *Even if you fall, for sure that's no disgrace.*
> *Just turn your eyes beyond the Cross; see our risen Jesus,*
> *Knowing that He died to give you eternal life.*
>
> *Come before Him, as the bridegroom, for the wedding day,*
> *Coming for a bride, adorned and ready, to hear Him say,*
> *"Come my beloved to the home where perfect peace lives;"*
> *We'll live and reign, eternally with holy angels.*
>
> *So dance and sing before the Lord, hallelujah;*
> *Lift up your voice; sing praises for His love eternal.*
> *Make a joyful noise, rejoice in His holy presence;*
> *Serve Him gladly with everything that is within you.*

Through the years of church, there would be these special weekends when outside singing groups and preachers would come into the village having special meetings—lots of good singing, lots of excitement for us children, and of course always a special time to taste some real good home baking, cooking from the people in the church. The meetings would draw people who had the same desire, same faith, and hope for the future. The church body was mostly Pentecostal by desire and experience so it became affiliated with the Pentecostal Assemblies Of Canada. For sure, there were also some visitors, with the same intention of praising and worshiping God. Sometimes when special meetings were at the church, outsiders might come out, somebody might get saved, somebody maybe got healed, and many more miracles happened, with the life-changing message of the gospel being preached.

Other Church Activities

Street Services At Glad Tidings church in Murray River, the street service was always a main part of the functioning of the believer services. In some of the early days, there would be a loudspeaker put outside the church, and people would stop, parking on the side of the road to listen to the service. Sometimes in the early 1950s, the group, especially under Herman Trentholm, would go to Montague and hold services on the sidewalk in the area where the parking lot now is between the Museum and Home Hardware. Sometimes people came and asked for help. A few times there were onlookers that may have been drinking and who would roar out slurred language from the passing cars, even cursing, acting crazy. So there I was at five or six years old, getting my feet wet in the "Go ye into all the world and preach the gospel" outreach programs. Of course we as children wouldn't do much except maybe get a chance to sing a little bit, alone, or with the group songs like Jesus Loves Me.

Here was that thread again weaving through my life in church and, in street services, which led me into the streets in Murray River, Montague, back and forth through the years. When the Pentecostal church started in Montague in the 1970's, they welcomed our involvement in their street services out in their parking lot. Then in Charlottetown, also through the 1960s and 1970s, I loved to participate, playing and singing, testifying, usually through the times when Trentholm and Cross were pastors. There would always be a great chance of sharing with people out on the street—those

My Early Years: Other Church Activities

who for some reason didn't want to or couldn't come into the church.

Home Prayer Meetings Around these years, we would have home prayer meetings in different peoples' homes from the church, something like today where we have prayer and Bible study groups in homes, called cell groups. I remember as a lad going to a couple of places, like Jim Richard's place in Abney, where the church group would have such desire to get together to study the Word of God. Also there would be a time of house prayer and study over at homes like the Moores. Of course as children, we would usually just hang around the doorsteps playing a little, with other children, yet you could still hear the shouts and praises of God's people while they had the meeting times there out in the country at people's homes. And especially to end the night off, if you liked, there would always be great home cooking and baking delights. Miracles would happen; people would be set free, believers gaining new freedom and having the joy of the Lord living within.

Camp Meetings There is a gospel camp over in Debert, Nova Scotia, where a lot of people took their summer vacations. Places where you could meet a lot of old friends and make some new ones too. Well the power of God would really visit that place. Even visit small children. There was a cookhouse where all the meals were prepared. Also the campgrounds had a canteen, which served the best hot dogs, that I can remember ever. But the biggest thing of it all were the services, especially as I got older. They had boys' and girls' youth camp and a teen camp, so you would stay in touch with your friends almost every year and see them at campmeeting time. The church was in the centre of the campground, up close to the gates for visitors for easy accessibility. When it was service time, there would always be an announcement over the loud speakers. During the service time, usually they would play the service over the air. When I first remember going there, the big bench seats were just nailed- together boards, the floors covered with wood shavings. There would be lots of the old time Pentecostal power falling. Some people would be falling on the floor, being filled with the Holy Ghost and power—some healing, lots of salvations, deliverance, and much more. Men involved at that time included I. D. Raymer, Sifton Irving.

There was a little children's church on the campgrounds where the whole service was adapted to the children's level of understanding. These dedicated people like Mr. Beasley, whom I remember especially because he was also the one who introduced me to Jesus. He told us this real tender story about God giving His Son who gave His life on the Cross for the sins of the whole world and he said that was for me too. So when he asked if anyone wanted to ask this Jesus into your heart, come up and get on your knees before Him and invite Him into your heart, I did, and never regretted it any of the days of my life. Camping always had a real important place in my heart because of all those nice things that happened there and the friends that I met then and some that I still meet today. This meeting at camp time was always such a memorable event. Every year we would enjoy the crafts and games when we were children, then also later the fun times and relationships fostered at the youth camp. Of course, the real big event of the summer was the family camp, for all ages from the very young to the grandparents. This was the time when the entire campground was filled with every activity you could plan followed by services filled with preaching, and singing—the ultimate investment of your time, worshipping God. Even Jimmy Snow, Hank Snow's son, preached there one year.

Church in Charlottetown Our family always had a real desire for the church, so when we moved around and eventually settled in Charlottetown, we stayed connected. There was always music. Mother and I would take it a step further, singing in church, with me playing the mandolin or guitar. Sometimes my mother and I would sing, or Mother and my Sister. My mother always had this real desire to be involved in the women's groups and the Sunday School as leader, my sister was on her way to Bible School in Ontario, in the early 1960s. Sometimes even when you could only walk, with the

My Early Years: Other Church Activities

snow so deep, we would still love the opportunity to trek on up the hill over the mile journey to the church. Sometimes we would be the only ones there, yet it was a lot of fun getting out in the dead of winter for the hike, with Jesus by our side all the way. We were there in the early days of Calvary Temple church. First, it was in a converted old chicken barn in Parkdale, with Vic Jackson as the preacher. Then the church started to grow, into a warm, loving, kind, dedicated group of Christians. It was the hard times of the early 1960`s, so every project was a big investment. At that time, I sure loved getting involved in Christmas concerts and whatever was going on in the church. Mother's example encouraged me to keep participating throughout my whole life. She loved to worship, and praise God through it all, to this day, That in itself I think deserves a real blessing from God for everyone who contributes all their time and effort to helping the church grow and stay strong. Just like the lighthouse keepers, the saints of God who stand behind and support God's compassionate appeal to mankind are measureless in their value to the world as a link to eternity and its reality.

Missions And Coffee Houses Even as a five-year-old boy there always was an awareness of the outreach appeals at the street meetings in Montague, the outdoor speakers at the church in Murray River, the outdoor service at the riverside baptisms. We were involved in door-to-door evangelism in Charlottetown even at age fourteen or so. When I started to travel to youth conventions in churches in Halifax, Nova Scotia, they would have a coffee house outreach where they would try to make friends with street people. Then, when I landed in Montreal, Quebec, there were a lot of mission appeals where you could sit in a little short service hearing the gospel in music and song, and then receive a hot meal and a place to lie down for the night. These places were found in Toronto and other centres out west, but in the 60's and 70's they became more like feeding stations for the people who found themselves out on the road travelling. All part of the Hippy, Baby-Boomer generation, travelling the roads in search of peace.

House of Angels

Music Influences

Music times We had some real fun times singing as a family, Dad, Mother, Sister and I, in our home with a guitar or two and maybe an accordion or a mouth organ. We usually could go on for hours, having a real fun time. My days with mother and Father involved some very interesting times, and I'm thankful for them all. At first when I was playing a little, I still knew enough about chording to play in church, a few years after we moved in to Charlottetown. I'd be playing every Sunday at church, then out at the street services. Also at the Christmas singing time, we would travel around carolling. At that time, as well as other times, we'd sing for the shut-ins, in seniors' homes like Beach Grove Inn, and at the hospitals. I loved singing with the choir. At that time Herman Trentholm had a radio recorded program on the air. We would all gather at the church for the choir practice and sing into a recording machine, which was then played on the radio later—having lots of fun times for Jesus.

As far as I can remember, Dad always had this desire for music (guitar, fiddle, piano, and whatever, but mainly guitar and fiddle). He always told about the absolute fun and good times they'd have around the old school house or community halls or wherever they would have their concerts, barn dances. You could always see an old guitar, or fiddle, around the house. Later on after conversion; with my mother they would sing and play together, mostly Dad on the regular guitar plus mouth organ, and Mother on the Hawaiian steel guitar. This sure was a good incentive for a kid to love the sound of music, see, and hear the live performance. Then of course he showed me the chords and at first, it seemed like a dream at 5 or 6 that I could ever learn to play Wild Wood Flower like Dad.

Well I loved the guitar most, at first not having one of my own but just playing my father or mother's guitar because there was always one around. Even though they weren't very expensive, it still made a sound, and that was a real attraction. Since my grandmother (Cecilia Bell, my father's mother) also used to play the steel guitar, every-

My Early Years: Music Influences

where I went there always was lots of music. It seemed all our contact people, friends, church, family, all loved to sing and play. Money wasn't very plentiful then so I never got my own guitar until I was around 10. I believe it was one of those *Simpson Sear*s guitars, around Christmas time.

Of course going to church and the participation with people playing and singing was one of the main sources of learning, along with a guitar course I tried one time, trying to learn some guitar chords. Still I would say the main thing that would help learning; was play, play, play, practice, practice, and practice. Through all these years, Dad would always love music. On our trips to Quebec, when we moved to Charlottetown, and wherever we went he would have a guitar or mouth organ always around to play and even entertain a little.

It always was amazing how we had this wonderful display of music around us all the time. From the times my father and mother would be playing and singing, my grandmother would be playing, and singing. Church, where I loved to go, would always have people singing and playing with their whole heart and soul into it. Even some would not be that professional, they made their performance worth a lot just because of their desire to play and sing. My Sister and I would have all the opportunity a kid would need to try to learn an instrument, play a tune, sing a song, and have a little fun doing it all. My Dad I believe at first had a *Harmony*—a black, acoustic guitar—which I played any time I could get hold of it. When my Dad was transferred to Quebec, I remember always the fun times of the parties; there would always be the fiddles, the guitars, all the singing. All around the county there was always this music, in many of the families, and my mother's family always had much music mixing in with all the family memories of childhood and people we were acquainted with.

Always there were special singers at church, also at conventions here at home on the Island and other places where we would drive when we had the transportation. Many specials, like Niles Thorn on the trumpet, Blackwood

House of Angels

Brothers Quartet, the Speer Family, the Learning family, and even in the last several years people like Gene McClellan and Marty Reno would play and sing, showing some of their fantastic singing and guitar playing. I remember Gene first about the early, 1960's, or 1970's, when he worked at Beach Grove Seniors Rehab Hospital Centre outside Charlottetown and came to church Sundays playing-singing such wonderful songs like Unworthy. Later on, I was fortunate enough to be invited to some of their jams in their own houses

My Guitar

My First Guitar

I remember when we moved into town, I was around 11, one Christmas I got my first guitar that was brand new, hard body electric, and amp, from Sears, I think. So the next step I figured would be, learn more chords, especially sharps and flats, etc., so I could play in church, where I loved to spend time. There was a guitar player there, Garth Birt, who really helped me a whole lot in this area with an ability to play better church music, country style, which he was

My Early Years: My Guitar

amazing at doing. Also the piano player (Mildred MacLean) would love to help in learning the flats and sharps, playing along with the songs. There always seemed to be this real desire just to do what I could do for Jesus since I was born again at seven and realized it was all making sense, that everything Jesus said was true, and making our relationship, that we together could make it. I've had many different kinds of instruments, but the guitar was definitely one of my favourites. I also liked trying to play the keyboard, harmonica, mandolin, fiddle, and many more. I've had many different guitars like *Harmony, Gibson, Pan, Yamaha, Fender, Framus, El Degas*, and the one I use now, a *Jean Larrivee*, a real nice little acoustic electric.

The saddest story about my guitar and me was one time, on my journeys, a friend with many guitars gave me this one when mine got smashed. It was a 12 string *El Degas* acoustic. That guitar pretty nearly played on its own. Everywhere I went, the guitar was my constant companion while I was a migrant worker out west. This guitar played such a big part in my life—so easy to play it took learning to the next level. It had such volume and quality of sound. Sometimes when the jobs were scarce, the guitar would fetch a few bucks in a pawnshop, getting some food and gas, etc., then for a couple bucks interest, I could retrieve the guitar next payday. In the last of my journeys out to the west coast, when I was coming back east, I was running short on funds. After the trip through the Rockies I landed in Calgary, nearly broke, so one night I found someone who would buy the guitar. With much regret, I sold it, retrieved more funds, headed back east. It sure did serve a purpose in my life; maybe someday I'll see it again, or at least one like it.

Wanderings

Bible College

Bible College seemed like it would be an answer to all the wanderings and questions I was having in my life. It wasn't that I thought I reached any big amount of perfection, but just a feeling about all my involvement in the Jesus type of things, like church, outreach, singing, etc. So back around the late 1960's I prayed, sought counsel, enquired, and applied to the Bible College.

Bible College 1968

Then the answer came back, accepted, which seemed to be the direction for my life. So I left the training in the trade school system, worked for some time to get some money, packed my bags, and away I went to college. The big problem seemed to be, I was from the country and liked my independence. So when the rules got really tight, there was a bit of a clash. I had a job in the community that took a lot of my time away from college; besides when I was there I would

Wanderings: Bible College

love going out with the bunch on weekend travels to sing and get involved in the music scene at concerts, etc. Anyway, all this moving out into the community gave me a little too much freedom, which I didn't want to lose. The school didn't think I was serious enough about the grades and started to demerit me. It was so trivial—even little things like, not being able to sleep at night, so I would walk with the night watchman whom I knew. Then the dean of men would drop by unexpectedly and give me more demerits. Eventually there were enough demerits to ask me to move on. I did.

On The Shore Of Destiny

Standing, watching, as the sea tides roll,
Seeing life before us just like a scroll,
Unfolding a plan; by our decisions we pay,
Forgetting not there are two paths in our destiny.

We have life to live, just as we choose.
Knowing one way we win, one way we lose,
When we shall come to our destiny's end,
Will faith remain, will faith still be our friend?

Alone in life, sometimes we will be,
Realizing time here is short as we can see,
With hope, one day, all things will be clear,
What we do now, we must decide and not fear.

In this frail temple of flesh, as we know,
We've embarked on a journey, choose it slow.
We will be changed, by eternity's plan;
To the shore of destiny, we'll sail with all man.

Now we're ready take one more step.

Working around there for a while, having not too much luck with finding a good job just night shift jobs like ABEX, or at Crayola Crayons, or service stations. So I decided to go back home and try getting a fresh grasp on life, so I headed

Sun Always Shines

back east from Peterborough Ontario, and the Bible college. The big problem was that this feeling of rejection still played with my emotions and gave problems with faith and belief, so I started to slip from the faith.

Jail Time

The very first time I remember having doubts about my faith, and listening to the Devil's lies and deceptions was one time I was slipping away from the truth, wasn't able to find good friends, losing interest in church and searching for love in all the wrong places. Hanging out with a rowdy bunch, partying. On a Saturday night sometimes friends and I would go to the places where a dance might be going on. Here we would push each other around, arm wrestling and acting careless. The normal thing for the management was calling the police and off to jail, locked up. After scuffling with the law, and causing a disturbance, I landed in jail for thirty days. This was so foreign to me, and no way could I fit

Wanderings: Close Calls

in this life style

Off to the exercise yard after dinner we would always be sent. Anything and anywhere would be better than in here, so I started to plan an escape. The food was like slop—nothing about this place would make you feel at home. The thought wouldn't go away. I wanted to get out. I saw an opportunity with some boxes piled by the fence, then the plan—climb up and over. With more watching and scanning for an opportunity, I went, jumped the fence and headed down the road, an escaped fugitive. I went to a restaurants near by ordered a shish-kabob (at last some real food) sat and ate, phoned a taxi out of town. At the time my only thought was, freedom. Then hitchhiking to the boat, and away. Still through all this, I didn't want to recognize that I was right in the middle of an all- out battle for my soul. On the one hand, there was God and the pure innocence of walking with Him, and on the other hand the call of the wild side. Yet somehow, I yielded control to the seductions and followed the way of going on my own without God involved, my own free will to choose. It was going from bad to worse. Here I was heading down the road somewhere over in Aulac, New Brunswick, sleeping in an empty train station on the hard old seats, leaving the loving family behind, heading out into the dark old night. It didn't take long for sense to kick in. I realized this was the wrong road and I should turn around. So I did, and headed back to the police for new charges and payment for my wrong. Through all this time my darling mother, the prayer warrior, and many friends from church all got down to business with God and asked for my help and guidance back to the right way. It happened—I got back to the Island and by a small miracle, the authorities figured I must have learned a lesson, and my time didn't get too much longer in jail after all.

Close Calls

When I look back, and remember the close calls with accidents or even disaster, it almost makes me think that I was accident prone, just looking for something to happen.

House of Angels

Now I don't really believe I was looking for accidents to happen, but the type of adventure I was looking for went through many dangerous roads. This is the part where the facts don't really seem to equal out. On the one hand I gave my heart to Jesus, I was going to church, playing and singing everywhere I could, the songs about God and His love. On the other hand I seemed to be drawn into these times of searching for my destiny—getting caught up in the need to belong and trying to find a place to fit in. This led me into a real maze of paths going in many different directions. Even through all this, I could feel God's compassionate appeal to me as a Father who cares and can help if we only turn to Him.

In The Valley Of Decision

Millions in the valley of decision,
Millions lost, for all eternity,
Who can go and lead them to safety?
So many wait, to be shown the way.

Confused and tired, they will be found guilty;
They do not know they must be born again.
In salvation alone, His peace will lead them,
Bringing Jesus on board, with no guilt or shame.

Surely, it's not only words that can reach them;
To show them God's love, in spirit we obey.
Their souls could be lost, maybe dying,
Without Jesus; He is the only way.

The love of God is always helping,
To the ones who daily seek His will,
For in Him is the true road leading
That has conquered the highest hill.

Hear the crying now, it's drawing nearer,
Of anguish, and pain, only the lost shall know.
In a short time, all things will be clearer;
We only have now, His compassion to show.

Wanderings: Drink

Drink

When we were very young, at the street meetings you could tell, from the way some of the people passing by were talking and acting, that they weren't themselves—they were probably drinking. Sometimes they were even outside the church, listening and shouting obscenities, or coming into the services trying to upset things.

It always seems so strange, even today, how a person can get so close to God, and still pursue the wild things of life. We must always remember, I believe, "Him that thinketh he standeth, take heed lest he fall." Now I try never being too sure of myself—just sure of Him

.I don't like to put a lot of emphasis on the times when I was straying away from God's path for my life. Yet to prove a point, I'll talk a little bit about playing around with the things of the world. When I would find my friends weren't interested in the things of God, and because of mean things happening—even in church—it was easy to go along with the crowds and have a little fun (or so it's called). There were times when they'd be having a few drinks and whatever, asking me to join in, so of course along I went for the ride.

Thinking back, going along seemed to come easy because I had seen many people do it when I was very young—just taking a drink and even getting drunk. This seemed to be the normal thing for them to do. Then there were the times when one of my uncles got so drunk, my father would have to put him out of the house, where we were all sitting and eating; then in a couple minutes, the uncle returned with a big knife smashing through the window in the house. So again, my father would have to deal with his own brother taken over by too much to drink. I'm sure the angels were there that night too, trying to defend against the terror of too much drinking and carelessness.

Wandering aimlessly through life with no hope wasn't in my plans. Yet I fell into that big hole a few times and don't really like even to think about it. The fact was that I was born again, and didn't plan to go this direction. I sure am overwhelmed that God can and will drag us out of any hole we may fall in, or even jump into. Especially since we can't do anything to deserve God's love, all we can do is accept it and thank Him for it. It really makes me seriously ponder—would God ever sanction an adventure on the risk side of life, where maybe you would even lose innocence for the sake of the knowledge about the wiles of the enemy? How might He act in the future, in your life, and the building of your testimony, good or bad? Then I realize that wouldn't be something we would have any say in anyway.

Bible College Again

Church instilled in me a real desire along with fantastic camp meeting times in Debert, a real desire to do more for God. He still was working on me, trying to get through to me about my direction in life. At one of the camp meetings, I had a real vision from God about preaching and working more for Him. It was an image of Him on the wall, while in a serious prayer meeting at Camp Debert in Nova Scotia, I felt it was Jesus beckoning me to follow Him, and do His will. Of course, I was aware of the life that God wants everyone to live, yet this seemed to be a more specific directive as to a pattern and a path for me to follow.

Within the next few weeks, through prayer and counselling, I decided to apply *again* for Bible College. The first time in the late sixties didn't take me all the way anywhere in particular, just caused confusion and discouragement, so it did seem strange to again be off and running in that direction. After applying, I was accepted and went for more Bible training. So now again, in the 1970s, I am at Bible school—*Eastern Pentecostal Bible College* in Ontario—studying to become a preacher. After failing once before, it seemed like I was attempting to climb Mount Everest, not wanting to quit though all Hell was breaking loose at times. I figured there must be more to this journey. I started to pray and seriously look for answers again. Being quite independent, I still had trouble fitting in.

After completing a second term of training, again there was that bit of strife. The Dean of Men again thought that it

Wanderings: Out West To Work

wasn't working out, so we had a talk with the President who agreed with him and asked me to leave the second time. So again, I am leaving Bible College.

Out West To Work

By Box Car I had a little money and knew there was an uncle of mine out in British Columbia, so off I go to get a job. Eventually, I arrived in Kamloops, British Columbia, where I had this telephone number to call and look for work. After much effort, there was not a lot of money left for pay phones. Not having any luck contacting this job prospect, I thought about my uncle who was out here in these parts working on a roofing business. I heard he had been hurt and I didn't have any way to contact him. Even the taxi company didn't know of him or his company, so it left me literally out in the cold--dead in the water. With the few cents I had left, I thought maybe I should get a good breakfast to start the day of not knowing for sure what would unfold as to where I would head next. Through the day searching around for contacts, for work or somebody who may know my uncle, or whatever, nothing worked out specifically. So here I was in Kamloops looking for these people and having no luck in finding them, out of money again and searching for a place to stay. Well, thank God for the hostels where at least you could get a place to sleep and a breakfast free.

A couple people I met in the hostel were French guys who told me about their plans to go out to Vancouver and look for work. Their way of travelling when they were broke was the boxcar on the back of the train that was travelling down the tracks empty anyway. The next morning after breakfast time they told me about the train times and so the three of us went to the best area where the train would slow down enough for a couple of seconds for a well-planned hop aboard the train. As the train came up the tracks, we were there watching and waiting for the dozens of cars to go by, towed by this pack of locomotives going clickety-clack down the railroad track. Then up ahead there was a bend in the tracks and city traffic, so the train had to slow almost to a walking speed. Just at the right second, we had the plan, throw the smaller one on, the he would haul and I would push the bigger guy up, then they would haul me aboard. So here we were on the box car ride of a lifetime right through the Rocky Mountains to the next stop which happened to be somewhere the other side of the mountains. On the boxcar, you could look out through the cracks and see all the majestic beauty of these mountains and on the curves looking ahead at this mile-long train going around these mountain paths—the view of a lifetime. Looking down, there must have been a half-mile drop; looking up there must have been a couple thousand feet of mountain stretching up to the sky, pointing to the heavens. The temperature on the train boxcars was below freezing, so in order to keep warm, with only one blanket, we would run around the boxcar jumping, walking, and doing exercises of sorts, while one person would lay under the blanket resting and then a change around every time someone would need a rest. We arrived in a little place about sixty or seventy miles outside Vancouver, hungry and desperate. We opened the boxcar door, and like a stampede of wild horses, out we jumped looking for freedom and food. We figured there was a place where people on the road could get help with a little food or other needs. We found the place and they gave us each a ten-dollar voucher for the grocery store. The two French guys and I went to the store and loaded up with a few things, bread, milk, pop, etc., and then parted ways. I went to the highway, hitching a ride towards Vancouver, and landed a ride in a beautiful little *Corvette Stingray* that flew down the big four-lane highway, getting us there in a short time.

Vancouver

So then upon arriving in Vancouver, basically all I had with me was a suitcase, a mouth organ to play a little music, and a few dollars in my pocket, looking for work. Of course, I didn't know anybody and didn't have any contacts here, so down the street I went walking with a little bag of belongings, searching for a place to stay. I was hoping to get my bearings for the morning when I would try to contact the

Wanderings: Vancouver

names of people to look for work, when I got the chance and phone.

Still this was the night and I needed a place to sleep, I met somebody who told me about a place in North Vancouver where transients stay who have been on the road with no funds. Here I had an encounter with the massive amount of people on the road. Also a close encounter with the wilder side of life; gangs would come into this transient house through the night to rape and plunder at will. Needless to say, nobody got too much sleep with these monsters of men throwing around these big hunting knives, sometimes at the floor, just to see the people sleeping there jump out of the way. That trip out west was turning into a nightmare. Still I had survived the night and didn't want to be on that floor a second night. So I asked around and found someone telling people go to the local welfare office, Maybe if you were lucky and had the patience to wait for eight or ten hours in a line, they might give you a room at a cheap little hotel with meal vouchers for a week, with the expectation that you'll find work. And again this was a nightmare, between the cockroaches running wild in the night having to sleep with the lights on to keep them out of the room and off the bed, to the sounds of Skid Row where some of the chronic abusers of drugs and different vices would be either dying or coughing or screaming through the night.

Fortunately if you look, sometimes you will find, and sure enough, the next couple of days led me to a glove factory where I was trained in pressing gloves after they were sewed together. So great, now I can get a room—a single, cheap little room but OK for a little while as long as I was making a little money and able to take care of myself. Even through these trying times, I could feel the thread that seemed to weave through my life—God watching and caring about what I got myself into.

Eventually I got another guitar and started meeting people who played and sang. So I joined in and jammed with them everywhere, learning a lot of things on the guitar. I was having a good time playing the guitar singing in coffee houses and at the same time joining other groups, bands, playing and singing everywhere, meeting people, sometimes even from bigger bands, just out around playing and jamming for fun. So, making lots of friends and backsliding a little spiritually, life went on.

On The Street Corners As I wandered out west, someone told me, take the guitar and go play on the street corners, and people would throw money in your hat, guitar case, or whatever you put out. So I did, and found a whole culture of performers playing for nickels and dimes or whatever they would throw in your container. One time I teamed up with an old native guy who played the fiddle like a real pro. We met outside town at a farm where we were picking fruit. Out there in the western provinces, work never was around everywhere, so you would have to travel from place to place looking for it. This travelling introduced me to migrant workers whom I met while picking cherries, apples, and peaches. These jobs with workers who came for the picking season and travelled back to warmer countries, like Mexico for their harvest seasons only provided a small amount of income.

So on the weekend we talked about this opportunity to play and jam on the street corners in Vancouver. We had a real time of jamming and getting quite a little bit of money for food or whatever. We made a lot of music together and a lot of friends, just hanging around listening to our stuff. Latter on after it got dark and colder, we parted ways. I met some other guys who were into rock and roll and asked me to jam with them in their place, so I did. Usually every day I would meet new people, some even from the East Coast. We would get together sharing food, a place to stay, sometimes help in finding work, and this led to the coffee house jamming.

Party Encounters—Wild Kind

When I travelled out west, I would always take my love for music with me and keep searching for another place to play and entertain. This one night down in Gastown, British Columbia, I was out street entertaining, getting some cash,

Wanderings: Party Encounters—Wild Kind

then into a few bars and restaurants looking for friends. One place I went into, I sat back in the corner at a little table, with my guitar, when the place shook like thunder. Looking for clues as to what was going on, people were observing the door area when through it came about thirty or forty of the roughest characters I've seen. They sat taking up nearly half the place and began to look for fun and frolic, something to eat and drink. Some of them looked over at me in the corner, and roared, "Hey, you know how to play that thing?" I motioned, "Yes." I had my guitar on my lap and teasing the strings a little. He roared, "Come on over and sing us something." So over I went and began my version of some rock and roll like *Johnny Be Good, Blue Swede Shoes, Bobby Magee, House Of The Rising Sun, Rock, Rock, Rock*. A couple of the big guys jumped up, went over to the jukebox, which had been offering a bit of competition, and yanked the cord out of the wall, roaring, "Play that thing, boy." So for an hour or two they had me entertaining them huffing and puffing and doing my thing. I had that still small voice of reasoning put pretty far back in my mind. Through the course of the evening and into the morning, after the fingers got numb from playing, voice croaking from the rocking, blasting sounds, the place was closing. Then we're all tumbling out into the streets, and one person told me about a party the next full moon at this farm out in the country, and said to come and bring my guitar.

Sure enough, the time rolled around and my desire to play and entertain gave me motivation to find the music party. There back in the country was an old farm, almost like an old outdoor rink or concert performance place. I arrived, parked my car, got my guitar and headed for the stage area. I stopped, chatting to a few people and started to get this funny feeling. Whoops! I believe I'm in the wrong place. These people were talking about doing someone serious harm, and it seemed like maybe it was me. When I made my presence known, coming close to where they were, several of them started coming towards me, and definitely didn't seem to appear like it was to shake my hand. When I turned around to leave, they started yelling and trying to get

House of Angels

hold of me, so I took off in the other direction like a fox on the run. Somehow, through all this confusion and the chasing—I was going under the vehicles, over some, maybe even through some—I managed to get to my car and floored it, jumping the ditch, taking out a piece of the fence, and flying down the highway. It was a miracle that I escaped that night. After that, I went back to the area close to the beaches, and all I could think about was that I was playing with fire, and in the back of my mind, that still small voice whispering, "Will you come home, before it's too late?"

My time in the west connected me to a lot of different people, some of whom were on drugs, and using them to get involved in the music scene. The problem was I usually tried out what my friends were trying and hung out a lot with them. Brave and bold, I figured, "Might as well try them out too." Back in the early 1970s, it was the normal thing to do—especially at the parties with the music I loved to play. The joint was rocking and the joints were being passed around, so of course here I went on the roller-coaster ride, trying out some of this new stuff. At that time I figured, everybody was into it and they all seemed cool, so here, let me try it too. The only problem with that was the God whom I did serve—I was going, going, gone, off course, but having too much fun to even notice. Here was all the rocking, the music blasting, everything just bouncing with excitement, and no one with even a thought about tomorrow. It seemed to be the same everywhere I went—Montreal, Toronto, Vancouver—the places were full of kids my age, in their teens and older, flying through this space where you would always feel safe no matter what you did, or what you took, because everybody was doing it, and that brought a real sense of safety. That of course was totally wrong. All around me was death and destruction. In one of the bars in Gastown, Vancouver, I remember times when there would be big fights, and someone would get killed, even the people I'd seen around selling drugs. On other occasions, I would see, sleeping out in the parks, an even younger group known as the runaways; even children as young as ten, with a bag over their head sniffing glue, to get a high and lay there all night

Wanderings: Party Encounters—Wild Kind

long, stoned out of their minds. You could even see them through the daytime in places where the older drunks and winos would hang out, prostituting themselves.

Lost Or Found

When it seems like the world is going to cave in,
When all around you falls apart with no mend,
When you've travelled on every road or so it might seem,
Then is the time to realize life is more than a dream.

When you've tried and failed so many times,
While travelling life's highway with so many different signs,
There's always a voice calling from inside,
Find the Rock in which we can hide.

While the storm rages and its fury- blast it shows,
The answers lie buried, no truth anywhere grows,
Destruction undetermined seems to take you astride,
That's the time, lost or found, we're on either side.

Lost or found is the message singing in my heart.
Is my life found in Jesus or still falling apart?
The time is now; behold, we're almost at the end;
We'll spend eternity in heaven or in hell because of sin.

End it All? Many things I only observed, like the drug pushing and other dangerous criminal activities and so lucky, or I should say thankful, that somehow I made it out of that scene in one piece. Yet in the night-time, I did some foolish things, some drugs, and a lot of music. I remember this one night, all alone, after partying a bit with some people, I went walking around the North Vancouver Bridge, which must have been a thousand or more feet high. It seemed to attract me so much, and I hadn't even noticed that God wasn't there as that still small voice anymore speaking, convicting me of the wrong. Where was my conscience? No, I wasn't really thinking about anything holy at all. So here I found myself up on this bridge, out in the middle, two or three o'clock in the morning, in the dark of the night, all alone, looking over the edge, feeling the strong wind tearing through my face. So strong! Hearing a voice in my head saying, "Jump, Jump, Many have run away from things before, so you too, jump." Back there in my mind or in some part of my memory the sound of the voices of my family, the people I've know, especially in church, saying, "Always serve God. The enemy will destroy, but God will give life." I'd hear the old familiar hymns like *"I wandered far away from God, but now I'm coming home"*. There on this cold dark night on the middle of a bridge 1500 feet up in the air, somehow those memories of childhood and friends gave me just barely enough strength and courage to walk away. It was so strange—even today I forget these memories quickly. Back then I tried to party on some more, but I couldn't seem to put my heart into it.

I was still part of the Hippy generation, just migrating around in the party mode, free love, free fun, free anything as long as you had some to give. Also like the moth millers in the summer, I was just migrating around with no real clear destiny. Eventually moths run into something that stops them, and likewise I had to run into quite a few things, before I slowed down enough to think about stopping. Thank God, He had enough patience to keep trying to get through to me, "You're on the wild side Stop and turn around before it's too late." His word always rings loud and clear, *"My spirit will not always strive with man; turn around and do what's right"* (while there is still time). I went away with that conviction inside my heart.

One Christmas at a high school in North Vancouver, they prepared an enormous Christmas party with the invitation to everybody in the area, "Come with food and help, or come and eat and help." They had a huge gym, full of every kind of food that you could think of—outside there was this giant spit and bonfire where they cooked whole sides of beef and pork. There were sure many different experiences. In Vancouver, there were so many beautiful parks. People would bring their musical instruments to them and play away, meeting a lot of like minded people and having a good time. No matter where you travel, people are in some ways

Wanderings: Through The Rockies Heading Home

the same.

As the time went on I bought an old *Dodge* car, drove it for a couple months, bought a guitar, traded the old *Dodge* car for a nice little four-door *Chevy*, which I drove back to Prince Edward Island and eventually sold.

Through The Rockies Heading Home

Each trip west I'd come home with a new mode of transportation. This time I started home with a beautiful little four-door *Chevrolet*, hardtop. It started out as a V8, but by the time I got home, it was only firing on two or three cylinders—found out later it was the spark plugs. Out on the Trans-Canada you don't have a lot of time to make any real lasting friendships. So I just drove and slept and sometimes ate. On the highway out west in the mountains, you would see so many massive sights, everywhere. One day I remember seeing this construction site where they were carving a side out of a mountain to make a road. It was amazing just driving up to the site from a distance. I could see the long line up of machines of every size and description—bull dozers, excavators, cranes, and trucks, of all types. There would be blasting and then hauling away of material they didn't use, grading, filling, and spreading of the new highway material, the pavement, or asphalt—sure a sight to behold. Driving through the Rockies, money was low and getting lower.

One very wet, foggy, cool night, with the rain just pouring down, I pulled into a service station. "Fill it up and check the oil." I ran to washrooms, then came back and paid for the gas. The attendant said everything else was all right, so down the road I drove. At the intersection by the service station there were three people hitchhiking, so I stopped and picked them up. Man it was pouring. Of course with the wet foggy weather, we needed the wipers, the defrost, and the lights (lt was night). The radio was playing, and here we were, the three hitchhikers and me rolling along. Within an hour or so, I noticed the lights seemed to be getting dimmer. Looking at the dashboard, I noticed the amp gauge was showing discharge, which of course meant the battery was going dead. I took measures turning the defroster off and winding down the windows a crack to see if that would keep the windows clear, which it did. Then of course, we didn't need the radio, so it went off. There wasn't too much else we could do except dim the lights, which would be two lights instead of four. So with every mountain, up and down, raining and pouring, the last thing I wanted to do was get out in this weather and look for the reason of the discharging, and of course the flashlight was dead anyway. There were no houses or any sign of another service station open anywhere, it must have been midnight or later, so what else was there to do out here except sleep with the bears, who didn't mind a bit of rain and came out every now and then just to remind you, "It's our country our here now people." The hitchhikers didn't know anything about mechanics and for sure that time of night everyone was getting tired anyway. I still remember that one last mountain. We were going up fine until the motor started to die out, so I just coasted the car around to a rest stop and parked. Out there in the mountains, there were no service stations in sight, so a person has to rely on their own abilities or go find help.

I started to remember things I learned at home from Dad. He worked around cars all his life, with me in tow much of the time; besides all my cousins usually were picking up this knowledge from their dads too, fixing and repairing, and we hung out together at different times in our life, and uncles in my family circle always had a bit of mechanical knowledge. But all that background didn't make a bit of difference right then at one o'clock in the morning with the rain pouring down. The motor just stopped and here we were. The thought came loud and clear into my mind—from that area where I still kind of hoped God's love might have been waiting for me to realize I can't escape from Him. The whole world is in the palms of His hands, but oh yeah, I remembered, I put all that in the back of my mind and wanted just to play around and have a little fun; He'll just wait and wait, until I finish my little playing around. But where was this playing around getting me, on the side of this

Wanderings: Through The Rockies Heading Home

giant mountain up here in the Rockies, the car dead on the side of the road?

I was thinking, "Would God lead a person through all this to prove His power for deliverance and salvation, even to me or to anyone one who calls on His name?" Oh boy! Into my mind poured overpowering thoughts, feelings, emotions, passions, fears, anxieties, and whatever else. Dozing off with no idea what to do but sleep, I remember this little voice somewhere in my being saying, "God, help," even the small thought about, I used to like Sunday School, I used to like singing those songs of praise, and now look at me, where am I going?

The next thing I remember, it was a bright morning. Up on the mountain, the bears were out getting into the garbage cans looking for breakfast, knocking them over, not finding anything, looking at us in the car, and after sniffing, determining there was no food there. Well that was another major hurdle crossed, except here we are, dead in the water, no tools, no mechanic, nobody anywhere in sight. Looking for volunteers—"Anyone want to go out and lift the hood to see if there's anything they can see that's wrong?" Of course, not just now. We sat there, for hours, until the bears decided to move along, and waited until we were sure; after all, we were on their turf and had to play by their rules.

The next few steps were to try coasting the car down the mountain and see if I could kick start the motor, but you still need a little charge in the battery. Driving the night before until it died, it was still dead. You can't keep the motor running, without a little charge of some kind. So I coasted down one side and up the other side of this mountain a couple times with no results, and running more and more out of coasting ability, too much friction and no ignition. I mentioned to the hikers, who were still with me, you might as well go back on the road—no sense waiting with me, I'll have to hitch a ride back to the garage, twenty miles or so and see about a boost for the battery or whatever could be done to fix the problem. So off they went hitching a ride in the other direction, while I went back down the road

House of Angels

hitching a ride to a service station. The operator came with the tow truck and tried a boost but with no luck, nothing happened; so he said he would go phone the other service station up the road in the other direction to come and tow the car there to check it out. The tow truck arrived; taking the car to their station, the mechanic took the car right in and told me the bad news, "It is the generator; it has had the brushes cut, looks intentional." After a new set of brushes, about seventy bucks, including the tow job, I was on my way again. The questions were going through my mind a mile a minute, "Who would have cut the brush wires, which are easily accessible right inside two slots at the back of the generator? It was just after I was in for gas last night the other side of the mountains." Well that was miles and miles of mountains back and there would probably be no way of getting someone to admit they might have just been trying to get the job of fixing the generator, trying to drum up some business. So I decided to keep heading east on this massive Number 1 highway, even with only ten or fifteen dollars in my pocket. After pulling into Calgary, I had to sell my beautiful guitar for a few more dollars to keep travelling as far as I could get heading home. So planning the next stop as Winnipeg, asking the people hitching a ride to pitch in on the gas, five or ten dollars each, with a full car load, we were heading of to Winnipeg.

The Dark Force I still wonder why God ever put up with my searching around for something to satisfy this longing within, and knowing way before this time—His love and mercy is the only answer.

Still on the road, feeling that dark force closing in and not wanting to acknowledge it, almost like playing with fire but not wanting to be burned. Playing my music and having fun, meeting friends everywhere, along with the few that were not friendly. Sometimes God's angels were the mercy carriers.

Out west there was no end to the opportunities where you could play and make music with people, but all the time more of these people were turning to drugs with no care

Wanderings: Through The Rockies Heading Home

whatsoever of their safety or future. I found myself wrestling with the question, "What am I doing? Do I want my life to just drop in this hole and end somewhere, somehow, whatever, whenever? Or do I want to head in the direction of faith in the future, hope in something better, trying to build a better tomorrow for myself, my friends, my family?"

Back on the road still trying to get all the pieces together so I could see the picture better, and ended up in Winnipeg, after driving from the west across a couple provinces on a couple bucks. I would pull up beside hitchhikers, roll the window down, and before I would open the door, I would yell out, "Heading east. Can you help with the gas? Then jump in." They all put in something for gas and we drove on down that road together, total strangers, all heading east, jammed into the car like sardines, with a similar destination. Through the night, stopping only for a couple hours of sleep, all sitting in the seats we travelled in. Somebody maybe made a sandwich; someone may have had a little water, so we all got by.

Winnipeg And On Finally arriving in Winnipeg, I started looking for a job, with not too much luck. Without money things were hard—it was in the late fall, and cold—especially at night. This led me to serious soul searching about where I was going and what I was doing way out here in the cold, no place to stay, no food.

That night I felt like going down town for a drive and stopping at a nice park just to see the sights. Well in the park were a few guys sitting around, who had this bottle they were sharing, and drinking. They asked me for a drive home, and when they found out I was just about out of gas, they said they had a solution; just drive them home to their place. There they got out of the car, coming back a few minutes later with a plastic jar and a hose, saying they had to take some out of their tank. So with a little gas to keep the motor running for heat they crawled back into the car, and we sat there and talked. Then looking at the time, after midnight, and realizing I start the new job in the morning, I said, "Guess I'll have to go get some sleep." Well this started a conversation about prejudice. They figured because I wanted to go, it meant I didn't like them, who they were. It was not true, but they argued, "Yes it was," I said, "No", and then they wanted to fight. In the old car I was driving, the front passenger door wouldn't open, so the only way he could get out was past me or over the back seat and out that way, the way he came in. This other guy was still in the back, so here we go again. Two or three o'clock in the morning, tired and sore, starting a new job maybe in the morning and everything, I just needed sleep. Anyway the guy in the front, in a flash grabbed me by the side; the other fellow in the back grabbed me around the neck and prepared for a fight, maybe taking the car or whatever they seemed to want. But God still cared somehow, and was close by, so I just bowed my head and said, "Help me Jesus, help me." Instantly the guy beside me took his hold off and brushed the area he was holding onto, the other guy in the back did the same, they both apologized, thanked me for the ride, and jumped out of the car in a flash.

Another day I was driving around, just searching for answers. I stopped at this little old house in the city, went inside and re-educated my life to Jesus, like when I first was born again at seven. Anyway, this person at the Youth for Christ was so kind; he took me to several places and helped me find a job, a place to get started again. Just before that all materialized, he introduced me to this friend he knew from church, who took me into his house and kept me for a few days, until I got work and a place to stay.

It was a time of rededication for my life and again asking Him for guidance in my journeys. After this came some more real-life experiences, like totally losing the serious smoking habit I picked up somewhere. One night after coming from church, driving down the road, I pulled out a smoke and tried to get it in my mouth and light it up. Oh my land what a smell! It was like something old, and dirty, stinking, and making me gag. I had to grab the package, with the one in my mouth, rip it up, and throw it out the window. There was no way I was going to need that in my life any more. Sure enough, when I got down on my knees and invited Jesus to

Wanderings: Through The Rockies Heading Home

come into my heart, the Holy Spirit was not going to stay around in an old stinky smoke stack, with all the coughing and spitting, and wheezing, etc. It was OK by me, sure don't need that vice in my life anyway, so good-bye to the smoking.

> ### Journey On
>
> Sailing many waters, here and there
> Mostly ships are finished here
> Everywhere the sun is setting low
> Even though we may sink here below.
>
> When faith will fail, hope is gone,
> The mind questions all things we've known,
> Leaning on trust is it placed firm enough,
> Storms of life destructive we're still journeying on.
>
> Then a voice loud and clear, go on, go on,
> You're getting closer, you are the Master's own,
> Don't leave your trust here in worry or care,
> Holding on to God, He is always there.
>
> While the storm rages in its fury,
> In our souls, the message is clear,
> Destruction could be the end to all things,
> We can be saved if to Him we stay near.
>
> Lost or found the message of my heart,
> Life for Jesus or just falling apart,
> The time is now good wind for sailing,
> Eternity in heaven where all is gain.

Yet still the call to go home was so strong I didn't feel any comfort zone there. So with these miracles happening I didn't want to move on but still I had the desire to go home and check things out. With a few more dollars, I made from the short-term employment I jumped aboard my old Chevy and headed home. Heading east, and went back to the Island, home sweet home. Of course, things had changed a bit, with some people moving, some people getting married. Still I had these wonderful parents to welcome me there.

Back Home

Of course, here on the Island the employment situation is always lean, so I tried to the best of my ability to land a job. The best I could do was service station work, farm work, truck driving, and many other labour intensive jobs like furniture moving. My dad and I tried various business ventures, including house painting, interior decorating, landscaping. I always had the music and all kinds of places to play at, especially church oriented functions and cable television. Around this time I was using some of the writing material I had adding up over a lifetime, some songs, some poems, some articles and more. I made a lot of friends in church at this time especially in a pastor called Bob Cross, who gave me an opportunity to perform some of the time in church. Also the cable television program, *Bill's Jamboree*, was a fun time where a lot of us local writer/singer people could get a chance to do our thing. These activities always helped with times of shortage in income, when you could find faith in family and friends who were on the same journey. Still there was this lack of good meaningful long-term employment.

So I travelled around the Atlantic Provinces, looking for work. I was in Halifax, Nova Scotia working at painting jobs, service station jobs, and nothing seemed to be very rewarding so I kept looking for alternatives. Going west the second time was in the 1970's, when I was in my twenties. Starting the whole journey of, I was travelling around the Atlantic provinces looking for work and wasn't finding any lasting jobs, just seasonal work.

In Newfoundland I couldn't find too much, just some day jobs with a fellow painting houses. So with not too much work, I either had to go to welfare for provision or move on again. Living in my vehicle around Saint John, not able to find work, making friends on the road, but still without money, I was seriously looking for new horizons.

Wanderings: On The Road Again

There was a Christian campground outside Saint John's, so I went there and stayed a couple days seeking my next move in my adventures of life. The campground had fantastic camp-meeting services with singing and preaching. Still I was not getting any prospects for work or involved in the churches.

On The Road Again

I met a fellow who told me about these jobs out west in Edmonton, Alberta. He gave me an address, and I let my adventuresome nature do the rest. Back in Grand Falls-Windsor, Newfoundland, I planned to sell the vehicle I was driving and hitchhike across to the ferry. From there I would get a train heading out west to this job interview. Sure enough, the car sold, so I packed what I could easily carry, and off I went, heading west.

Hitchhiking was a real experience, meeting all kinds of different people and thanking God for protection. A few rides only went a few miles, while some went all the way to another town, which was great. For example, this one ride took me into the country where I met another person heading down the road heading west, and another ride took me to the next town, which I believe was Corner Brook.

Then a fellow driving by in a pick-up truck, stopped and asked me "Are you hungry?" Of course, I was, so he said, "Jump in the back," and he took me home with Him where his wife had this most delicious home cooked meal with all the trimmings. Feeling like a well-fed hired hand, he dropped me of at the intersection and away I go again, thumb in the air feet on the ground, seeking for adventure.

Getting close to dark, a tiny little Volkswagen pulls up, opens the door, and into this big cloud of smoke I climbed. The guys aboard this ride were riding high; the smoke was coming from a handful of weed. They were roaring, laughing, and smoking, asking if I would like to participate. I said *No* and waited anxiously for the boat terminal to appear. At the ferry terminal I thanked them very much for the ride and got away. I purchased a sleeping pass for the ferry and boarded for the crossing to North Sydney. I slept most of the way. Arriving in Cape Breton, I purchased a ticket on the passenger train heading west with the funds left from selling the car. Next stop was Truro. There were signs a real big storm of some kind had just passed through. It was around the first of July. There were trees down and a lot of stuff blown everywhere. But since the train was leaving in an hour, I never strayed too far.

Train Heading West So the same thing was happening, here I was on the road, then the train, always just moving on. The desire to travel came naturally, maybe somewhat inspired by a life growing up that included a lot of visiting people, along with all the different places we moved. Everywhere I went, of course my favourite travelling companion were musical instruments—mostly the guitar and the mouth organ. At first mainly travelling just here in the Atlantic Provinces and playing in with other groups who were putting on concerts, and home parties. There I would get an opportunity to sing and play a special. Then later on looking for work I ventured out west with the desire to play, play, play. Off course, trying to travel light and sometimes hitchhiking, with no vehicle of my own, either the guitar stayed home or I had to sell it to get funds for the journey. So when these travelling days came, the harmonica (mouth organ) was so much easier to carry.

So off I go again on the highway of life seeking my destiny. The old train seems slow sometimes, but that's good; you always can jump off if you have a change of plans, at the next stop. Not so, for sure, in an airplane, so I preferred the train. Anyway, the train stops lots, picking up and dropping passengers off. This can be very boring if you're in a hurry, which I really wasn't. It was just nice to get a chance to see and meet different people. Into New Brunswick, across to Quebec, Montreal, Ontario, Toronto, and on we go. All along these tracks I wandered—so many people, so many places, and everybody with a mission of some kind, maybe sometimes not even sure of it. So all through the big cities, where sometimes we changed train cars, but still going west, we

Wanderings: On The Road Again

were on our way. Through the prairies—Manitoba, Saskatchewan, and into Alberta. Here there were a lot of native people getting on and off the train, using this as a regular means of transportation. There were always many people getting on the train with musical instruments. Many times, you could hear them play, and I loved trying to play along, meeting friends everywhere. At night, it was a quiet kind of time for reflection—dark, lights on the train low, many people sleeping a little, and here we all were heading down the tracks to our destiny. Sometimes I took out my harmonica and played quietly, seeking my plans for tomorrow—trying to keep peace in the picture all the way.

One place in the backwoods of Saskatchewan, the train had to stop because of the heat was warping the metal in the train tracks. To avoid a derail, they stopped until dark to let the tracks cool down—three or four hours. I remember this especially because at this same time, the air conditioning unit stopped working, and the metal train cars were almost cooking—the temperature up to a 100 degrees or more. Some places on the train there were doors to open. The warning was, "Don't leave the train. We don't know the exact time we'll be moving." For sure, away back here in the woods up north and west you don't want to be left alone, especially not without proper provision.

On the train, there was a cook-car restaurant where everybody was getting a meal occasionally. They had the car painted red so with the temperature rising a hundred degrees and more, the air conditioner was broke, there was no breeze, the kitchen staff busy cooking meals adding to the temperature, you could almost melt just walking in that direction. We would all try to get close to the open doors or windows if we could find room.

I landed in Edmonton Alberta, Canada from the train trip out west to find work and didn't find very much in the way of good employment. This place was where I had the encounter with the house of Angels where I got delivered from death, by the hand of God. There didn't seem to be any place here for me to fit in so I planned to head back east.

House of Angels

Heading Back East I couldn't find my uncle in Kamloops, so I worked my way back east on the farms. I eventually ended up in the Rosetown area—at a big wheat farm covering thousands of acres, where they raised and trained wild horses. Here I drove trucks, swathers, and other farm equipment. We would cut down the rows of grain and double them up with an older-type tractor that ran on propane. Then my job would be to drive the trucks to the big grain elevators for dumping—night and day. It was a long, tiresome type of work.

Determined

I've made up my mind no longer to be
In a boat of confusion upon life's stormy sea;
Now won't last forever, yet eternity will;
Home for us all with Jesus, doing well.

Determination is the lifeline holding on to the fact-
One standing for the cross and never turning back.
Lasting throughout the ages forever, now to see
Is it true determination lasting for eternity;

For me I choose to follow in the footsteps of our God
Know the path He'll guide our feet on this path we trod,
Always having the same problems, Jesus had when here before,
To persevere always onward, towards heavens open door.

Determined, yes, determined forever in my mind,
Following, always wanting more of God to find.
That others, precious Jesus, will see that they can
Serve with joy and gladness our Master and His Plan.

I took part in a roundup, first of the cows, then the bull that was on the loose, but the biggest roundup of them all was rounding up the wild horses. The farmer would use his truck and trusty dog flying through the field, dodging the prairie dog holes, and letting the dog out to correct the animals' direction towards the pen when they went astray. It

Wanderings: On The Road Again

was always a danger, running the horses too hard because of these holes in which they could break a leg quite easily and have to be put down. The planked horse pens were about ten feet tall. Here they put the horses to await saddle breaking. His wife would do that, or some people would buy the horses as they were. As soon as I left that farm, I headed on down the road, hitchhiking to the next farm and worked for a couple weeks taking care of pigs and chickens.

One night after supper, going to bed I was awakened by a strange sound. I got up and looked outside, but couldn't hear anything. There were lights on in the building where they weld and fix mechanical things, but there wasn't anything going on, so I went back to bed. I was awakened again by this big image of a red figure which I guessed was a demon, so needless to say at that time I was again in need of help from God, and the only message I was getting this time was, "It is time to move on." A few days after all this, I did.

Still I had this desire to go home so off I go, purchased a car and headed down the road. This trip, which was my second time out west, the furthest I went was Edmonton, Alberta, then coming back through Saskatchewan, then Manitoba and so on. The only problem this time was this car I purchased had transmission and motor problems, so out on the road you sure don't want those things to deal with, but I felt so desperate this time to head home I was willing to take a chance and try anyway. One place they put a new filter in the transmission, which fixed it temporarily, but then the motor started smoking bad, so in New Brunswick I was putting in a quart of oil every thirty miles with both the motor and transmission quitting. Finally, the car died, and after some thought, since it was getting close to dark, I went to a house and phoned my parents on the Island to see if they would come and pick me up. Sure enough, they said, "Yes," so I waited, and in the meantime, I was introduced to someone who wanted to buy the car right on the road, as is. I made the sale right there, waited for my parents, and got home again, only this time with no guitar and just a few clothes.

House of Angels

Back Home Again

The job situation on the Island hasn't improved much in the last fifty years, just little bits of growth here and there. When a handful of jobs come, usually they're for professionals, or there's only one for every ten unemployed. when I got home, there were only the potato- harvest jobs, picking tobacco jobs, or make-your-own-business jobs. I got to thinking about education—what I would like to do and what I could do. That led me to an employment office and an aptitude test, which opened all kinds of different doors. Around 1980 I was accepted into Holland College, Summerside, for a chef's course. This led to work at hotels, hospital, and other self-employment- like restaurants. All this time I tried to stay very much involved in music with a lot of thanks from a lot of people, a lot of volunteering, at seniors homes, benefits, caleighs, and at church two, three, to seven times a week, which I loved so very much, and still do today. At this time, I was playing the piano more and trying to learn new styles, playing for myself as well as for church services.

In 1985, after looking for love in so many places I finally met a little lady from the hills of Cape Breton, Nova Scotia, Mrs. Rose Bell, formerly, MacQueen, and after a while we decided to marry. I asked, she replied, "Yes," and so it happened. Here we were, pledging the rest of our lives to love and cherish each other, and look what happened, it worked! Still together twenty three years later with two babies who have both grown to men and pursuing their own destiny, both workers, and life goes on, into the future with only God knowing for sure what we can be certain of.

Thoughts

I Can't Help But Share

Where will you spend eternity?
Are you concerned about your soul?
Do you know or do you doubt if you even have one?

Have you ever asked yourself these questions or others similar? I have many times through my life so far wondered if realistically there was a part of my life here that would live eternally in one of two places, either Heaven or Hell.

Reading the words of God, I've found in so many places that man does have an eternal destination in either of these two places, either heaven or hell. For those who are saved, we can read about it in 1 Peter 1:4 *"...Incorruptible and undefiled and that faded not away, preserved in heaven for you...."*

Hallelujah! For such a wonderful promise given unto men to accept God and have a home in heaven according to His word, or we can reject Him and lose our chance of going to heaven for a home in hell, where we will spend all eternity. The eternal destination in hell, where, the Word of God states, is prepared for the devil and his angels, when God has deemed the time is right, this will also be the place for those who totally reject God and the price paid on the cross at Calvary for us by His Son so that we may have eternal life.

One day at the judgement. (Matt. 25:41) *Then shall He say also unto them on the left hand, depart from Me, ye cursed, into everlasting fire prepared for the devil and his angels.* Oh! Friend there are definitely two eternal destinations to consider, where we will go when this life is over here on earth; choose wisely while there is still time to prepare. The time is coming, according to God's word, when we'll all be judged how we've lived our life here on earth and if we have accepted God and His Son. The way of salvation is for all mankind. Jesus Christ, God's Son said in the Bible, (1 John 14 6) *"I am the way, the truth, and the life; no man cometh unto the Father but by Me."* He is the way of salvation; we must be saved through Him and, I believe, by His precious blood He shed at Calvary, our sins can be washed away.

Knowing we have sinned, according to Romans 3:23, *"For all have sinned and come short, of the glory of God,"* *"If we confess our sins He is faithful and just to forgive us our sins and to cleanse us from all unrighteousness,"* and *"Believing on the Lord Jesus Christ and confessing by mouth to others and believing in our heart God has raised Him from the dead, we shall be saved."*

Whoa! How can this not be a good deal? A home in heaven, peace forever more, living without any problems, or troubles, seeing Jesus, all the saints of old, our departed loved ones, joy forever and soooo much more. I thank God for saving a sinner such as me. One day I wandered in sin but praise God, now I'm saved and know beyond even the shadow of a doubt that I'm bound for heaven and will see Jesus Christ this Saviour of mine (and hopefully yours too) waiting with out-stretched arms, waiting to welcome home his children. If these words mean something to you, I hope you'll read these Bible verses and become a Christian confessing them; then we'll all be part of the big family of God.

Hope

Jesus said, *"Neither do I condemn thee, go and sin no more."* (John 8:11) Really sobering words, especially in a world where there seems to be so much prejudice, racism, and even hatred, for many people, and even sometimes it just seems so completely unfair how we can hate and judge one another, when we're just human too. We're living in a world today with the signs everywhere, feelings of anxiety, hurt, misuse, deceit, deception, etc. We all could add some thing to the list, and probably everyday there will be more and more new pieces added to this picture, even though it brings such pain and hurt. Within us, we all usually want peace and love, but sometimes we get caught up in a web of corruption and deceit. Within us, we've probably heard the

Thoughts: Hope

story about Christmas, *"Peace on earth, good will toward all men,"* (Luke 2: 14), also in Luke 24:36. Then we look outside wondering today, "Where is the earth going? Where did this wonderful peace go?"

I Love You

When I say I love You,
All the stars shine so bright.
When I tell You I need You,
Almost, every day and night,

Through the night and the day,
All my cares are gone away.
You're right there when I need someone
Through the storms and trials.

I love You, I love You,
I really, really love You.

All my tomorrows will now be OK,
Just because You've come to stay.
No storms too long or mountains too high,
Nor rivers too wide; in your presence I'll abide.

I love You, I love You,
You make the light shine so bright.

When those dark clouds rain everywhere,
They block the sun, bring us care,
Loads sometimes heavy, yet You're still right there;
Lord, help us and our burdens share.

I love You, I love You,
I really, really love You.

Well I think Jesus made it clear, Romans 3:11,12. and Romans 3:23. *"We were all born and shapen in sin,"* so this was the reason Jesus came to give us a way of coming home to the Father's side, where we can live forever with Him, in that land far beyond all earth's troubles and trials. *"For the* kingdom of God is not meat and drink but righteousness, peace and joy in the Holy Spirit." (Romans 14:17). So we sure do have a way of escaping the things of this earth that keep us in bondage, especially to the flesh. We do not have to hold these things inside; we can go to Jesus in prayer, and like a kind, good, caring Father He always will be there for us, to show us mercy and grace. "For God so loved the world that He gave His only begotten Son, that whosoever believeth in Him shall not perish but have everlasting life." (John 3:16). He will not betray us (our trust) or privacy, but instead show us real love and concern.

Nature Of Man

2 Corinthians 5:17 *"Therefore if any man were in Christ, he is a new creature: old things are passed away; behold all things are become new."*

Galatians 6:15 *"For in Christ Jesus neither circumcision availeth any thing, nor uncircumcision, but a new creature."*

Ephesians 4:24 *"And that ye put on the new man, which after God is created in righteousness and true holiness"*

It seemed through all my encounters with life and the harsh realities, that there are always different ways to accept things. Usually when they are going your way, it's not a very hard thing to live with yourself and the people around you, but then when the road starts to go rocky, things aren't going your way, all kinds of reactions happen. There is always this idea, and even facts, that we can work through some things, maybe even accept some things as being something we can't change, and of course hoping to acknowledge the difference. I would think these are the times when our nature really gets involved. Did we get a desire to be really like Jesus when we were *born again*? Or did we really see the need to change as much as we could? Is there a possibility, we maybe dealing with some things that are vain?

Ecclesiastes 5:10 *"He that loveth silver shall not be satisfied with silver; nor he that loveth abundance with increase; this is also vanity.* "It just seems to me that there are so many things in life that can be our choosing; to do it this

Thoughts: Nature Of Man

way or do it that way, and sometimes maybe not God's way.

Life just has so many decisions we have to make. Once we decide to seek salvation; coming to God, accepting Him as our Master then the only right way to make decisions is to follow God all the way—praying to Him to lead us into the right choices. Yet always there is the will, or nature to help us make decisions, or even confuse us in the decision making process, in life, and then we have to live with the choices we make. Joshua 24:15 *"But for me and my house, we will serve the Lord."*

That was one verse, or this one seems to be interesting along the line of choosing: Matthew 6:24 *"No one can serve two masters; either he will hate the one and love the other or he will be devoted to the one and despise the other. You cannot serve both God and money."*

The only real point I'm trying to make here is, many times the things we choose to do in life, work either for our advantage or for our disadvantage. You've seen the immediate results in some of the stories I've been telling—times when God in His mercy sent angels to help me in my extreme times of troubles. We'll have to wait until we stand before God the Righteous Judge after our time here on earth before we can really evaluate our decisions. Or even after life passes by and we look back later on in life, we can evaluate the circumstances that happened to us with more clarity.

Can man win his life? Or is it up to him? Can he choose to damn his soul, maybe by the decisions he makes? And eventually send his soul to hell. Is it possible to be really in control of your nature—would you want to be? Can man really be shaped by the material things around us, even like sounds hearing, sights, and the things we see, etc. For sure from the very beginning God would have the choice to either give to man no chance of choosing, or give him a free will, where we can choose freely, like *"whom we are going to serve,"* our destiny and eventually where we will spend eternity. As the Bible so many times tells us, if we choose foolishly, we will stimulate our carnal nature and then leave ourselves open to the disadvantage of losing out with God.

House of Angels

Many times, we find the two choices running neck to neck, and we either choose to live in the spiritual realm or the carnal realm. We live in our salvation, thinking about things above, or to our damnation we go on living for things below.

Winter and Spring

Hoping

Since all time goes on, day by day,
Sunshine arrives, some things feel OK.
It grows things, warms things thawing the snow,
We start again, and away we go.

Yet, soon, this grass that grew, fades away,
Then darkness we see ends another day.
Time keeps passing, the time of man,
We're all in it together, this great big plan.

Just the passing of seasons, we see them go,
Whether spring, summer, fall, or the time of snow.
All scheduled in time, sequestered so fine,
We're in this Plan; we've an appointed time.

So, let's admire the sun, stars, moon, them all;
We're all here together, trying to stand tall.
Seeding, growing, harvest, rules all things well,
Hope, could lie dormant, let's grasp it and tell.

Thoughts: Nature Of Man

Amazing God

Has time stopped? We wonder what is real,
The emotion, passion, and wonder we feel,
Waiting for someone to return again,
Then home to that land, no more sin

Now it's raining, we can feel His presence,
From our hearts we pour it all out to Him.
Help us Lord, give us calm assurance,
You're coming, You're here, You live within.

They constantly bow and worship,
Crying, holy, holy, before the throne;
We too someday can join them,
Singing in worship, before the Lamb.

Pathway To Home

Through different paths I had to roam,
I am now found on the one leading home.
In many trials I may have been found;
God's love was there, His Spirit so sound.

God sent his best; Jesus stood the test,
To save from sin, made the haven of rest.
Time will always be, throughout eternity;
In Jesus we have love, joy, peace, and liberty.

Here in this life some things seem to say
Jesus is the Word and His promises will stay.
I know He lives and will forever stand;
I've placed my hand in His nail-scarred hand.

Now life is a journey on this pathway I roam,
With heaven in sight as our eternal home,
Friends walk beside me, friends I adore,
One more step in life and closer to heavens door.

House of Angels

> ### Gonna Climb That Mountain
>
> *Gonna climb that mountain, with my Lord,*
> *Gonna climb that big mountain, with my Lord*
> *Gonna climb this here mountain, with my Lord,*
> *All the way, up to heaven, all the way, with my Lord.*
>
> *My soul it is seeking, for the Lord.*
> *Soil in this world is rocky, where seeds are sowed,*
> *And even thorns and thistles sometimes only show;*
> *Gotta keep on climbing with help from the Lord.*
>
> *Up there's the sunshine, yes all the time.*
> *Such sweet communion, in this heart of mine,*
> *Precious Jesus, lover of my soul.*
> *Lord and Master, take full control.*
>
> *He gives us good things, while living here below,*
> *Joy in the Spirit, where His blessings flow.*
> *We can shout for the Master, our Everlasting King;*
> *Peace always in His presence we can always sing.*
>
> *Oh yes, let's determine, never looking back,*
> *Keep on climbing that mountain, right on track;*
> *See the angels coming, on our journey home,*
> *Ministering servants sent by God to never leave us alone.*

The Judgement

Have you ever thought about judgement, law, or lawlessness? So many times in our world, there is the need for laws, to help us live in a land with some peace in it. A decision is made by a judge to punish people who break the laws set for us to live by. For sure, I believe it's always better if we have rules and some regulations to live by. Even nature has laws, and if we don't work with nature then nature always shows us who's in charge.

Have you ever thought about God? Like in the Bible, it tells us that one day we will all stand before God. We will be held accountable for the things we have done in the body,

Thoughts: The Judgement

with Jesus taking all our sins away if we ask Him, sincerely believing that He can. Then as mere human beings, we can keep on living, trying to do our best, having a responsibility to try, and knowing that God will help and forgive if we need Him to. Otherwise, if no repentance is made, we will be held accountable for our sinful acts.

Just today, I was driving and noticed the big beautiful sunshine in its amazing array of colours. This also God will judge all one day along with all nature—2 Peter 3:11,12. Involving the end time and God purifying all things by fire. Then the children of God will go to that land where we will have need of nothing, not even the light because the Lamb is the light—Revelation 21:23 and Revelation 22:5, *"To that city where, the Lamb is the light."* As God's word will be until the very end and beyond. We too will have to stand in the end. The Almighty God will determine where we will spend eternity, telling us, either Heaven, or Hell. It is words such as this that makes me realize we'll really stand one day before the Almighty God, meeting Him on the hills of glory. It brings a holy reverence and fear to know all the things awaiting us. But all the time we have Jesus, our blessed Saviour, who will stand for us and say He has washed our sins away and forgives us our trespasses. In the Holy Bible I have in my hands, it says God promised that, *"Whosoever will, let him come and drink of the waters of life freely"* (Revelation 22:17). God also is love and showed how much by sending us a way of escape if we believe in Him. So then, we can have eternal life either in Heaven or in Hell. In joy and peace; or otherwise lost, just by accepting or rejecting His Son, Jesus Christ.

My best friend in the whole world, my Dad, had to go to heaven in 1998, which left a real big hole in our life, but we who remain live with the expectancy that we shall meet again. Now I still live to play more music and long for another opportunity to do it.

All the encounters I've had and still have each day now have me living totally for God. There is never any more desire to turn back now, especially when I see the closing days all around us and the facts everywhere that, if those before us talked about this soon return of our Lord and Saviour, then it must be all the closer now, since so much more time has passed by. *"Be ready, for in such an hour as you think not, then Jesus comes."* (Matthew 24:44).

> *Living Eternally*
>
> *We will dance for all eternity,*
> *The day we hear death has been destroyed,*
> *When finally we can grasp living forever,*
> *The angels proclaim praises around His throne.*
> *The blood washed saints of God claimed for his own,*
>
> *Resurrected to praise Him in peace and joy in that kingdom.*
> *The last enemy God will finally destroy,*
> *So we can live forevermore.*
> *To live eternally in love peace and joy,*
> *Sit at the Master's table inside that open door.*
>
> *To see Jesus and know Him, face to face.*
> *Meeting the saints and loved ones gone on before.*
> *Being with the angels and all heaven to adore.*
> *You notice time flies and waits for no one.*
>
> *Just keeps turning the pages as we live day by day.*
> *We can only imagine what we would change*
> *If time were controlled by us mere mortals,*
> *Yet it keeps on passing by.*
>
> *We must occupy, or else we'll look at it when it's all gone,*
> *And look back with hope and not with regret.*

More than ever, I believe that through our life we can see the results living day by day, and how it relates to our upbringing. When I was very young, there were always friends around, and lots of friendly people, so it came naturally for me to try and get to know people, making new friends. Since I was saved at a very young age, everything I did was connected to God and His will for my life. I believe

Thoughts: The Judgement

He has a plan for every one of us that we can walk in. Finding Him pleased with our actions as His children. Likewise as children, our earthly father wouldn't do harm to His children because they make mistakes and do wrong. So likewise if we choose God, then His word shows us the way to go and the promises we have in Him, and He won't do harm to His children. That's when I really noticed the intervention in peoples' lives including mine, when God's presence was so precious, and how He would send His angels to watch over us and *"Protect us lest we should dash our foot against a stone."* (Psalm; 91:12). So when we make our choice to walk in His way, that's when we see all kinds of miracles happening. I believe it's never too late for us to make a complete commitment to Him—to see these principles in action. The lifeline is there, all we have to do is reach out grab it, and the Father will send His angels, taking us to safety. Sometimes we may wonder even a little, when we see a person living so carelessly; they'll be lost. Then we hear God's words saying, *"It is not My will that any should perish but that all may come to repentance."* (2 Peter 3:9) or *"Whosoever should call upon the name of the Lord should be saved."* It all seems quite clear to me—even more as I get older—that He was there all the time and showing me His *"Blessed assurance Jesus is mine, oh what a foretaste of glory divine"* as the old hymn of the faith declares.

Well the whole story keeps showing me, I'm just part of a very large body—the body of believers. One may be a foot, a hand, an ear, eye, nose, leg, etc. How necessary every part is to make the body complete! Every part has such a useful function to keep all things intact and healthy. One person said one time, "Yah church, I've had enough of that. All I feel there is pride, ego, judgement, control, etc. Man, let me get out of this place to a place of freedom, joy, and celebration— a place where all men are recognised as being created equal." All this love, joy, peace, is without debt, just given to mankind by His love, all we have to do is accept it. Jesus paid it all. It's free since He said, *"Whosoever the son sets free is free indeed,"* (John 8:36), and in Him, our Father, Shepherd, Lord, and Friend. He said *"Come unto Me all ye*

House of Angels

who are weary and heavy-laden (carrying a big weight), and I will give you rest." (Matthew 11:28-30, So many verses, so many ways He just wants to love us and give us a reason to believe. He's the Saviour for us, the Shepard for the sheep, He's the Doctor when we're sick, He's the Helper to the helpless, our Banker when we're broke. He's the Saviour, the Lamb of God, and comes to us sinners needing a way out of this mess, needing forgiveness. He forgives.

He Shall Return

Someday He's coming again,
Someday He's coming again,
His power to discern,
Someday He's coming again.

The Bible many times it tells us,
Prepare to meet thy Lord,
But so many still wait,
Why do they hesitate,
When Jesus is coming again.

Loved ones now gone on before us,
The Lord takes care of His own,
If only we could see,
They would tell to you and me,
All the glories of heaven we'll share.

So now we must toil on further,
Waiting for the trumpet to sound;
In the skies He will appear,
Then He'll dry every tear,
Yes, my friend, He's coming again.

All this time we are responsible; we helped nail Him to the old rugged cross, we who from the fall in the garden of Eden have been born and shapen in iniquity. Yes, He, the Lamb of God, shed His blood at Calvary so we can go free, free, free, from the curse, from the bondage of sin, hallelujah forevermore.

Thoughts: Prayer And Meditation

> *Power Prayer*
>
> *Resurrection power, in me, oh Lord, in me, oh Lord*
> *Restoring love, in me, oh lord, in me, oh Lord.*
>
> *Healing, cleansing, washed in Your blood.*
> *Healing, cleansing, washed in Your blood.*
>
> *Freedom, oh lord! Give us freedom,*
> *Freedom, oh lord! Give us freedom,*
>
> *Jesus, Saviour and Lord, our Master,*
> *Jesus, Saviour and Lord, our Master.*
>
> *Take our sins, break our sins, break these chains.*
> *Set captives free, oh Lord! Including me.*
>
> *Jesus! Jesus! Jesus! Jesus! Jesus!*
> *Saving power, saving power, full and free.*
> *All bondage must go, through Your Name, we will see.*
>
> *From these snares and pit's, love will never quit*
> *Break any vice that keeps us bound by Your power, oh Lord!*
>
> *You're King Of Kings, Lord Of Lords; rule in me,*
> *In me, oh Lord, through me, oh Lord, to set us free.*
>
> *Coming back, like Your word said, for your own,*
> *For Your church, Your people, who believe in You.*
>
> *Your own dear children, Your own precious body.*
> *Who are Your bride, meeting the bridegroom in the sky.*
>
> *We, in the Spirit have been washed, have been cleansed,*
> *Through the Lamb Of God! All set free through the Lamb Of God!*

Prayer And Meditation

There is always this struggle between good and evil for the souls of mankind, for the control of this world, influencing mankind to do what they do. Powers of evil, sin, and darkness must be broken in the name of Jesus, Son Of God, Master, Saviour, and Deliverer. In that name—the name of Jesus—God will come in His power and break these chains that bind us, restore our joy, heal our body, and restore the sweet communion between the Father and us, if we earnestly seek Him with all our hearts. The Lamb Of God, slain from the very foundation of the earth, can rekindle the flame within. When we pray this in Jesus' Name, we experience cleansing, renewing, strength to go with the Gospel everywhere. With the revival spirit, we go on praying, seeking His face. *"If my people, who are called by my name, will humble themselves, and seek my face, then will I hear from heaven and heal their land."* (1 Chronicles 7:14). Holy Spirit flow, flow across this land, filling your people Oh God! Moving in love, power, taking away all the stress, tension, sinful ways, giving joy, peace, dance, and celebration, praise, worship, and truth. All the good things of God are raising up a people of power. A mighty army of love for God, showing the way in a world of lost and dying souls. To shine Your light, Jesus, let Your Spirit move, right now! Holy Spirit, move, in my life, in our lives, letting the glory of God move through us and move through the world. Show that the real hope and answer for our problems today is found in serving Jesus.

God Sees Us

God's eye is always watching us through our good times and bad, whether we do good or evil. He sees all men even though some maybe rebel to the point of trying to cover their eyes and escape from God watching them. He may allow them to feel confidence (trying to rebel) against Him and maybe they'll even have a superficial feeling of having stopped God's ability to see them and have escaped His response. Yet we cannot stop God in any way from seeing us or responding to our hurts and needs. Or eventually God punishing those who persist in disobeying Him, rather than choosing to live at peace. He can automatically see all the earth, because of His omni-present power, unhindered by anything, beholding man and all the actions we take, as

Thoughts: God Sees Us

mere human beings, created a little lower than the angels. We will all stand one day and give account, for the lives we've lived here on earth. This most beautiful planet created for us in the original creation, lovely, peaceful—a home for all men to keep the faith, and obey His pattern for life.

As in the original creation in the Garden of Eden, man was created to have fellowship with God. So in the beginning of all things we had this relationship between God and man. Along the way, it seems some have badly slipped and now have a seared conscience (doing things their own way), not caring anything about a real and existing God. Still as a kind Saviour and Father, He always provides a way of keeping a good relationship with Him, and having forgiveness from sin. At first through animal sacrifices, then the great sacrifice—Jesus on the cross-at Calvary. There was always a way of escaping the wrath of God and maintaining a good relationship between God and man. We can walk close to Him and become part of the great big family of God. Yes, I believe that God made the earth. In the beginning, He put man here to create and cultivate, be fruitful and multiply. He gave us the breath of life and yet in the Garden man chose to disobey. So as children of our original human parents we inherit the results of this original sin. However, He did not leave us without a way of escape—He sent His Son, Jesus who willingly gave us a chance of redemption by believing in Him. Now if we choose Him, we can become part of the family of God and be content when realizing God is watching us in love, reserving the punishment only for those who persist in doing evil. Yet still in this age of grace and mercy He waits, giving all a chance of repentance, turning to Him.

Life can take on this form of suspense, where all you see is this bag full of troubles and trying to find a way to deal with them. Really we can just, *"Cast all our cares on Him for He careth for us."* I can't help but see this big hand which I would like to see as being God reaching down through the clouds (even on sunny days) and taking hold of this lifeline (like mercy, grace or, hope, could be). We are holding onto the other end, maybe even wrapping it around us (this lifeline) so when He pulls us out of our troubles we don't slip off the other end, to easily anyway, until the rescue is complete. Like we're overboard in this big storm in the waters, waves over our heads, just barely staying afloat, when we hear this voice crying out, *"Grab the lifeline,"* of course we grab for the line wrapping it around us if we still have the strength and get rescued from the stormy deep. So when you're in times of testing or even troubles, don't forget to take the time to look up, reach out and take hold of that loving hand of God who is reaching out to us. With prayer always and sincerely believing that He's there and will help.

Living God and Resurrection Power

From the garden to the trial, He walked the road with none to share. From the cross to the tomb, all our burdens were with Him there. Redemption was planned and resurrection power, for this sin-cursed world of ours, missing so much love and compassion, if only we could show it to everybody that this Jesus can be everybody's Loving Father, and all go to that home of peace love and joy, in the Holy Spirit.

He cried with a loud voice and gave up the ghost. An unseen hand rent the veil from the top to the bottom. The earth quaked and the rocks were rent. Saints arose out of the graves and visited many in the Holy City.

After His resurrection, all power, He reclaimed keys of the grave, death and Hell, so we all may be saved. The power of the living God will heal the church today. After His resurrection, now we may have that same power today. *"All hail,"* (Matthew 28:9-20) spoke the Master when from death He arose. Go ye now and tell the others of their Christ who arose. And meet me there on the mountain where he said all power is given to me and to you in my name always, now rejoice you've been set free.

Go ye therefore and teach all nations baptizing them in the name of the Father and of the Son and of the Holy Ghost. Teaching them to observe all things, whatsoever I have commanded you, and lo, I am with you always, even unto the ends of the world, amen.

Thy Face Oh Lord

The face of my Lord I want to see,
The face of Him who died for me,
When on heaven's shore we do arrive,
Stand at last by our Saviour's side

Glowing in glorious splendour I see
The face of Him who died for me.
With only love in His eyes, we can tell
He gave His life to save us from Hell.

This face they marred at Calvary
Will shine forth as the sun for eternity.
Though the scars we see through our earthly eye,
God will cleanse them all in that sweet by and bye.

Let Your power show through the darkness,
Taking away all fear, giving us peace.
While there's still time here to seek truth and life,
May we never doubt without asking for truth.

Let us journey on together
Through the very changing stormy weather
Until we all cross over the finish line,
No one left out of the joys yet to win.

When Your lightning flashes,
Let it speak forth in hope.
Oh, let it dance on the injustices of man
To set Your people free in all this land.

Conclusion

> ### I'll Serve Jesus
>
> I'm going to tell about my Jesus
> Everywhere I go.
> I'm going to shout aloud His praises,
> Through this entire world below.
>
> Since I met the Master,
> And He saved my soul,
> I want to tell the whole world,
> That Jesus can make you whole.
>
> I'm going to walk with Jesus, hand in hand every day,
> I'm going to depend wholly on Him, every mile of the way.
> Until that hour when I see Him, behold Him face to face,
> I'll keep trusting alone in Jesus and His saving grace.
>
> I'm getting ready every day, to make that special trip.
> I've got my hands on the lifeline, trusting I'll never slip.
> With my life on the altar, with Jesus I'll always be,
> Safe, secure, and protected, both now and through eternity.

The Goal

I believe, what my soul seeks for is having Jesus, in control of my whole life. To be accountable for His love seen In our lives. *"To every man there's given an equal measure of faith,"* (Matthew 17:20). Do we nourish this faith, *"faith as small as a grain of mustard seed"* which can help us move mountains, or do we try to ignore what the Saviour of our lives wants us to do. *"By grace we are saved through faith, not of works lest any man should boast"* (Ephesians 2:8). Faith first, and growing faith as we follow Jesus letting Him take the wheel, seeing and believing more and more everyday in His mighty acts. Sometimes we see the forces that can come against the soul, leaving hurt, or confusion, maybe scarring and bruising, resulting in living a life very weak, not the way Jesus wants us to live. He said He would

Conclusion: The Goal

be with us through the storm. *"Trust And Obey"* the words of the song says, and, *"Casting all our cares on Him" "Like a good earthly father gives good things to his children that ask Him, so our heavenly Father gives good things to His children that ask Him" "His strength is made perfect in our weakness,"* (2 Corinthians 12:9). There, you have it, we come, we receive, and He'll always be by our side, giving us strength to go on.

The Hand Of God

The hand of God will always be
Guiding and leading, through the Spirit to see.
We may have left Him before; now we earnestly pray
To live for Him day by day.

The hand of God will forever be
Powerful enough to deliver thee,
Not because of works that we have done,
But for reason of peace God sent His Son.

Salvation alone body, mind, and soul,
With His own precious blood, we are made whole.
Still looking for room in Him to grow
With His love, He showed us there's so much more;

This Spirit which is God can always be found
In a heart of love He's always around;
The sins of life will then be washed away.
The power of God—sin He will always slay.

I believe there are forces continually trying to seduce the soul, to sin and then convince us we're defeated. But of course I believe if we immediately come to our Heavenly Father and confess, *"Confess our sin, He is faithful and just to forgive us our sin, and to cleanse us from all unrighteousness"* (1 John 1:9). He will forgive us, and give us strength to go on. You can see the flags flying; on the one side, the forces of evil and on the other side, the victor, the Lord

House of Angels

Jesus, whom I choose to serve, if I want to be, on the winning side.

> ### Earth's Final Sundown
>
> When our labour is done, the day's rest has begun,
> We wait 'till tomorrow brings that new day dawn.
> Though we sweat or we toil on the sea or the soil,
> We'll wait 'till it's past, the sundown at last.
>
> When we wake in the morning, sleep in the night.
> We know everything in Jesus will be all right,
> We look in the Bible, the answers to survive,
> Put our trust in Jesus, on Calvary He died.
>
> Jesus Christ, you've set us free,
> Saving our soul, a real mystery.
> Oh the marvellous love He's given to man,
> Went away in a cloud and likewise He's coming again.
>
> Carry the torch for the Lord; show the light across the land,
> Live what's right day and night for God, no time for delay;
> God's great mercy on us here, even those gone astray,
> Deception may overcome some; serving God is the only way.
>
> Where we are today following Christ all the way,
> Close by His side, never going astray.
> Follow the Word that is real, trust in it every day,
> See Him standing by the throne, "Judgment's coming," hear Him say.
>
> Earth's final sundown coming soon, then all things change.
> We see the cross before us where Jesus paid the sacrifice.
> The battle belongs to Him, from now 'till eternity,
> Angels from the throne descending to help His children, set them free.

Because of this warfare, I know the enemy will be defeated and put in the bottomless pit *"where the only sound*

Conclusion: The Goal

Final Sundown

will be weeping and wailing and the gnashing of teeth" (Matthew 13:49, 50). What a terrible day to think about, I also know that all who live by lying, deceiving, killing, destroying, and all these terrible destructive things, will find their place there also. There's just no sense in even taking a chance— we have the gift of grace given us; reach out and receive it. Then we can live a life sheltered in the big powerful, kind, loving, arms of God where we can live at rest from the cares of trying to make it on our own.

Outside the will of God seems to be the weakest place to live, where we can be tossed about throughout our whole lifetime, where the raging storms of life can smash against us, trying to topple us over into the raging seas. Casting aside all of this world's sin and strife, turn to Jesus and there we'll find the haven of rest.

Time will have to yield one day to the Master of it all when He takes full control for all mankind to see. Whether our goals, hopes and dreams, have been completed in this world or only just begun, if the motives are right and our intentions are pure, we'll carry them all to Jesus and lay them at His feet casting all our crowns at His feet. *"For me to live is Christ (Jesus), and to die with Christ (Jesus) is gain."* (Philippians 1:21). So our far better choice, I believe is to belong to the bride of Christ, standing on the promises, and never letting go of our hold on the lifeline.

Conclusion: The Goal

After All

After it all, something's grow strangely dim;
It makes you wonder still how fragile I am,
Life, which I felt inside, doesn't seem like a place you can hide;
The first step where you place your faith
Will be the origin of our eternal state.

Walk on towards tomorrow, no other way;
It's a path we all must travel, seek a new day.
For sunshine some would gamble, some may even run away.
We're here. Look optimistic, hold on.
Reason within, for in it all there is a plan.

So fragile, this human creation of mankind,
Held in suspense for all tomorrow's dreams.
Can we guess about destination? Escape the path of isolation?
All we've learned through life and our journey
To try for gold. I hope we all can really see.

Now looking back some times were stormy,
Yet sailing on, still more seas to roam,
Thy presence lingers like new- discovered mountains.
We can climb, accomplishing new things;
He'll send the help, justice will be served.

www.ingramcontent.com/pod-product-compliance
Ingram Content Group UK Ltd.
Pitfield, Milton Keynes, MK11 3LW, UK
UKHW041950230426
12048UKWH00008B/249